W9-ABI-190

Modern Critical Views

Chinua Achebe
Henry Adams
Aeschylus
S. Y. Agnon
Edward Albee
Raphael Alberti
Louisa May Alcott
A. R. Ammons
Sherwood Anderson
Aristophanes
Matthew Arnold
Antonin Artaud
John Ashbery
Margaret Atwood
W. H. Auden
Jane Austen
Isaac Babel
Sir Francis Bacon
James Baldwin
Honoré de Balzac
John Barth
Donald Barthelme
Charles Baudelaire
Simone de Beauvoir
Samuel Beckett
Saul Bellow
Thomas Berger
John Berryman
The Bible
Elizabeth Bishop
William Blake
Giovanni Boccaccio
Heinrich Böll
Jorge Luis Borges
Elizabeth Bowen
Bertolt Brecht
The Brontës
Charles Brockden Brown
Sterling Brown
Robert Browning
Martin Buber
John Bunyan
Anthony Burgess
Kenneth Burke
Robert Burns
William Burroughs
George Gordon, Lord
   Byron
Pedro Calderón de la Barca
Italo Calvino
Albert Camus
Canadian Poetry: Modern
   and Contemporary
Canadian Poetry through
   E. J. Pratt
Thomas Carlyle
Alejo Carpentier
Lewis Carroll
Willa Cather
Louis-Ferdinand Céline
Miguel de Cervantes

Geoffrey Chaucer
John Cheever
Anton Chekhov
Kate Chopin
Chrétien de Troyes
Agatha Christie
Samuel Taylor Coleridge
Colette
William Congreve & the
   Restoration Dramatists
Joseph Conrad
Contemporary Poets
James Fenimore Cooper
Pierre Corneille
Julio Cortázar
Hart Crane
Stephen Crane
e. e. cummings
Dante
Robertson Davies
Daniel Defoe
Philip K. Dick
Charles Dickens
James Dickey
Emily Dickinson
Denis Diderot
Isak Dinesen
E. L. Doctorow
John Donne & the
   Seventeenth-Century
   Metaphysical Poets
John Dos Passos
Fyodor Dostoevsky
Frederick Douglass
Theodore Dreiser
John Dryden
W. E. B. Du Bois
Lawrence Durrell
George Eliot
T. S. Eliot
Elizabethan Dramatists
Ralph Ellison
Ralph Waldo Emerson
Euripides
William Faulkner
Henry Fielding
F. Scott Fitzgerald
Gustave Flaubert
E. M. Forster
John Fowles
Sigmund Freud
Robert Frost
Northrop Frye
Carlos Fuentes
William Gaddis
Federico García Lorca
Gabriel García Márquez
André Gide
W. S. Gilbert
Allen Ginsberg
J. W. von Goethe

Nikolai Gogol
William Golding
Oliver Goldsmith
Mary Gordon
Günther Grass
Robert Graves
Graham Greene
Thomas Hardy
Nathaniel Hawthorne
William Hazlitt
H. D.
Seamus Heaney
Lillian Hellman
Ernest Hemingway
Hermann Hesse
Geoffrey Hill
Friedrich Hölderlin
Homer
A. D. Hope
Gerard Manley Hopkins
Horace
A. E. Housman
William Dean Howells
Langston Hughes
Ted Hughes
Victor Hugo
Zora Neale Hurston
Aldous Huxley
Henrik Ibsen
Eugène Ionesco
Washington Irving
Henry James
Dr. Samuel Johnson and
   James Boswell
Ben Jonson
James Joyce
Carl Gustav Jung
Franz Kafka
Yasonari Kawabata
John Keats
Søren Kierkegaard
Rudyard Kipling
Melanie Klein
Heinrich von Kleist
Philip Larkin
D. H. Lawrence
John le Carré
Ursula K. Le Guin
Giacomo Leopardi
Doris Lessing
Sinclair Lewis
Jack London
Robert Lowell
Malcolm Lowry
Carson McCullers
Norman Mailer
Bernard Malamud
Stéphane Mallarmé
Sir Thomas Malory
André Malraux
Thomas Mann

Modern Critical Views

Modern Critical Views

ROBERT FROST

Edited and with an introduction by
Harold Bloom
Sterling Professor of the Humanities
Yale University

CHELSEA HOUSE PUBLISHERS
New York ◊ Philadelphia

Printed and bound in the United States of America

10   9   8   7

∞ The paper used in this publication meets the minimum
requirements of the American National Standard for
Permanence of Paper for Printed Library Materials, Z39.48–
1984.

Library of Congress Cataloging-in-Publication Data
Robert Frost.
    (Modern critical views)
    Bibliography: p.
    Includes index.
    Contents: Frost's enigmaticl reserve / Robert
Pack—The redemptive imagination / Frank Lentricchia
—Choices / Richard Poirier—[etc.]
    1. Frost, Robert, 1874– 1963—Criticism and
interpretation. I. Bloom, Harold. II. Series.
PS3511.R94Z9158   1986   811'.54   86–4220
ISBN 0–87754–626–6

Contents

Editor's Note

This book gathers together a representative selection of the best criticism devoted to the poetry of Robert Frost, arranged in the chronological order of its original publication. I am grateful to Susan Lasher for her assistance in editing this volume.

The introduction explores some aspects of the influence of Emerson upon Frost, particularly in their shared gnosis of "the American religion." Robert Pack, Frostian poet and critic, begins the chronological sequence with a meditation upon Frost's deliberate distancing or "enigmatical reserve" in regard to his own poems. In a parallel discussion, Frank Lentricchia argues that Frost's sense of the limits of redemption that a poem can perform marks a crucial distance between the High Romantic theory of the imagination and a more limited modern sense of reduced imaginative possibility.

Richard Poirier, who seems to me Frost's canonical critic, traces the poet's crucial early choices that made him so distinctive a voice in American tradition. Poirier's conclusions are supported implicitly by Marie Borroff's sensitive discussion of Frost's language, with its rugged ability to achieve elevation by rising out of a basic simplicity.

Two very different approaches to the relation between Wordsworth and Frost are made by Sydney Lea and David Bromwich. Lea makes of the relation a subtle study in "purged aspiration," while Bromwich, in the broader context of adding Wallace Stevens to this contrast between poets, achieves the valid insight that Wordsworth differs most crucially from Frost and Stevens because of the presence, in his greatest poems, of figures "radically unassimilable to himself," such as the old Cumberland beggar, and the many other vagrants, beggars, lost children, bereaved women, and deranged souls who people the greatest modern poet's universe of feeling.

This book concludes with two recent essays that consider Frost's achievement in the context provided by contemporary advanced literary criticism. Herbert Marks, writing on Frost's elitist "counter-intelligence," finds in the poet an aggressive technique that enhances displacement or loss, while denying that Frost was a Gnostic, in an argument that I acknowledge as stimulating my own introduction to considerable disagreement. Finally, Charles Berger, in an essay published for the first time in this volume, studies Frost as a mythologist of origins, skeptical and supple, and cannily capable of achieving a saving distance from the fictions of his own poetic sources. The emphasis upon "Directive" as a central poem, by both Marks and Berger, repeats a concern for the poem that is expressed throughout this book, from the introduction to Berger's conclusion. It seems clear that Frost issued both a perpetual challenge and an ongoing directive to critics in his great poem, which will always stimulate fresh generations of commentary.

Introduction

Frost—at his frequent best—rivals Wallace Stevens as the great American poet of this century. He does not much resemble Stevens, ultimately for reasons that have little to do with the "essential gaudiness" of much early Stevens, or even with the austere clairvoyance of the later Stevens, poet of "The Auroras of Autumn" and "The Rock." Both of those aspects of Stevens rise from a powerful, barely repressed influence-relationship to Whitman, a poet who scarcely affected Frost. Indeed, Frost's uniqueness among modern American poets of real eminence partly stems from his independence of Whitman. Eliot, Stevens, Pound, Hart Crane, W. C. Williams, Roethke— all have complex links to Whitman, covert in Eliot and in Stevens. Frost (in this like Whitman himself) is the son of Emerson, of the harsher Emerson that we begin only now to recover. Any deep reader of Frost understands why the poet of "Two Tramps in Mud Time" and "Directive" seriously judged Emerson's "Uriel" to be "the greatest Western poem yet." "Uriel's voice of cherub scorn," once referred to by Frost as "Emersonian scorn," is the essential mode of irony favored throughout Frost's poetry.

"Uriel" is Emerson's own irreverent allegory of the controversy set off by his "Divinity School Address." There are certainly passages in the poem that seem to have been written by Frost and not by Emerson:

> The young deities discussed
> Laws of form, and metre just,
> Orb, quintessence, and sunbeams,
> What subsisteth, and what seems.
> One, with low tones that decide,
> And doubt and reverend use defied,
> With a look that solved the sphere,
> And stirred the devils everywhere,
> Gave his sentiment divine

> Against the being of a line.
> "Line in nature is not found;
> Unit and universe are round;
> In vain produced, all rays return;
> Evil will bless, and ice will burn."

At the center of this is Emerson's law of Compensation: "Nothing is got for nothing," as Emerson phrased it later, in the remorseless essay "Power," in his *The Conduct of Life*. The darker Emersonian essays— "Experience," "Power," "Circles," "Fate," "Illusions"— read like manifestos for Frost's poetry. Richard Poirier has demonstrated this in some detail, and I follow him here in emphasizing how pervasive and crucial the affinity between Emerson and Freud tends to be. If there is a particular motto that states the dialectic of Frost's best poems, then it is to be found in a formulation of Emerson's "Self-Reliance."

> Life only avails, not the having lived. Power ceases in the instant
> of repose; it resides in the moment of transition from a past to
> a new state, in the shooting of the gulf, in the darting to an aim.

One thinks of the extraordinary early poem "The Wood-Pile" (1914), where the poet, "out walking in the frozen swamp one gray day," comes upon "a cord of maple, cut and split / and piled" and then abandoned:

> I thought that only
> Someone who lived in turning to fresh tasks
> Could so forget his handiwork on which
> He spent himself, the labor of his ax,
> And leave it there far from a useful fireplace
> To warm the frozen swamp as best it could
> With the slow smokeless burning of decay.

That "slow smokeless burning" is the metaphor for Emerson's "instant of repose," where power ceases. Frost's restless turnings are his most Emersonian moments, American and agonistic. His Job, in *A Masque of Reason*, puzzling over God's Reason, deliberately relates Jehovah's dialectic to that of Emerson's "Uriel":

> Yet I suppose what seems to us confusion
> Is not confusion, but the form of forms,
> The serpent's tail stuck down the serpent's throat,
> Which is the symbol of eternity
> And also of the way all things come round,

> Or of how rays return upon themselves,
> To quote the greatest Western poem yet.
> Though I hold rays deteriorate to nothing:
> First white, then red, then ultrared, then out.

Job's last two lines here mark Frost's characteristic swerve away from Emerson, except that Emerson is the most difficult of fathers to evade, having been always so subtly evasive himself. Frost's authentic nihilism is considerable, but is surpassed by "Fate" in *The Conduct of Life*, and by a grand more-than-Frostian late entry in Emerson's *Journals*, set down in the autumn of 1866, when the sage felt burned to the socket by the intensities he had experienced during the Civil War:

> There may be two or three or four steps, according to the genius
> of each, but for every seeing soul there are two absorbing facts,—
> *I and the Abyss.*

Frost's religion, as a poet, was the American religion that Emerson founded. A latecomer exegete of that religion, I once offered its credo as *Everything that can be broken should be broken*, a Gnostic motto that eminently suits Frost's poetry, where God, whether in *A Masque of Reason*, *A Masque of Mercy*, or in "Once by the Pacific," is clearly animated neither by reason nor mercy but only by the blind necessities of being the Demiurge:

> It looked as if a night of dark intent
> Was coming, and not only a night, an age.
> Someone had better be prepared for rage.
> There would be more than ocean-water broken
> Before God's last *Put out the Light* was spoken.

A God who echoes Othello at his most murderous is himself also crazed by jealousy. Frost's celebrated negativity is a secularized negative theology, almost wholly derived from Emerson, insofar as it was not purely temperamental. Slyly aware of it, Frost used it as the occasion for lovely jokes, as in the marvelous "Two Tramps in Mud Time":

> The water for which we may have to look
> In summertime with a witching wand,
> In every wheelrut's now a brook,
> In every print of a hoof a pond.
> Be glad of water, but don't forget
> The lurking frost in the earth beneath

That will steal forth after the sun is set
And show on the water its crystal teeth.

"Two Tramps in Mud Time" hymns the Emersonian negativity of refusing to identify yourself with any work, in order instead to achieve the Gnostic identity of the knower with what is known, when the sparks of the Alien God or true Workman stream through you. A shrewd Gnostic, Frost refuses to lament confusion, though he also will not follow Whitman in celebrating it. In Emerson's "Uriel," confusion precedes the dimming of that Miltonic archangel of the sun, who withers from a sad self-knowledge. Uriel-Emerson (for which read Frost) is himself not responsible for engendering the confusion, which results from the failure of nerve suffered by the heavenly powers when they hear Uriel proclaim that "all rays return; / Evil will bless, and ice will burn":

As Uriel spoke with piercing eye,
A shudder ran around the sky;
The stern old war-gods shook their heads,
The seraphs frowned from myrtle-beds;
Seemed to the holy festival
The rash word boded ill to all;
The balance-beam of Fate was bent;
The bounds of good and ill were rent;
Strong Hades could not keep his own,
But all slid to confusion.

"Confusion" is a mixing or pouring together of entities that would be better off if kept apart. Whether instinctively or overtly, both Emerson and Frost seem to have known that the Indo-European root of "confusion" originally meant "to pour a libation," as if to the gods. Frost's "form of forms," or confusion which is not confusion, identified by him with the Emersonian rays returning upon themselves, is a kind of libation poured out to the Alien God, as in the trope that concludes his great poem "Directive":

Here are your waters and your watering place.
Drink and be whole again beyond confusion.

II

"Directive" is Frost's poem of poems or form of forms, a meditation whose rays perpetually return upon themselves. "All things come round," even our mental confusion as we blunder morally, since the Demiurge is nothing but a moral blunderer. Frost shares the fine Emersonian wildness or freedom, the savage strength of the essay "Power" that suggests a way of being whole beyond Fate, of arriving at an end to circlings, at a resolution to all the Emersonian turnings that see unity, and yet behold divisions: "The world is mathematical, and has no casualty, in all its vast and flowing curve." "Directive" appears to be the poem in which Frost measures the lot, and forgives himself the lot, and perhaps even casts out remorse. In some sense, it was the poem he always wrote and rewrote, in a revisionary process present already in *A Boy's Will* (1913) but not fully worked out until *Steeple Bush* (1947), where "Directive" was published, when Frost was seventy-three. "The Demiurge's Laugh" in *A Boy's Will* features a mocking demonic derision at the self-realization that "what I hunted was no true god."

North of Boston (1914) has its most memorable poem in the famous "After Apple-Picking," a gracious hymn to the necessity of yielding up the quest, of clambering down from one's "long two-pointed [ladder] sticking through a tree / Toward heaven still." Frost's subtlest of perspectivizings is the true center of the poem:

> I cannot rub the strangeness from my sight
> I got from looking through a pane of glass
> I skimmed this morning from the drinking trough
> And held against the world of hoary grass.
> It melted, and I let it fall and break.

The sheet of ice is a lens upon irreality, but so are Frost's own eyes, or anyone's, in his cosmos. This supposed nature poet represents his harsh landscapes as a full version of the Gnostic *kenoma*, the cosmological emptiness into which we have been thrown by the mocking Demiurge. This is the world of *Mountain Interval* (1916), where "the broken moon" is preferred to the dimmed sun, where the oven bird sings of "that other fall we name the fall," and where the birches:

> shed crystal shells
> Shattering and avalanching on the snow crust—
> Such heaps of broken glass to sweep away
> You'd think the inner dome of heaven had fallen.

Mountain Interval abounds in images of the shattering of human ties, and of humans, as in the horrifying "Out, Out—." But it would be redundant to conduct an overview of all Frost's volumes in pursuit of an experiential darkness that never is dispelled. A measurer of stone walls, as Frost names himself in the remarkable "A Star in a Stoneboat," is never going to be surprised that life is a sensible emptiness. The demiurgic pattern of "Design," with its "assorted characters of death and blight," is the rule in Frost. There are a few exceptions, but they give Frost parodies, rather than poems.

Frost wrote the concluding and conclusive Emersonian irony for all his work in the allegorical "A Cabin in the Clearing," the set-piece of *In the Clearing* (1962), published for his eighty-eighth birthday, less than a year before his death. Mist and Smoke, guardian wraiths and counterparts, eavesdrop on the unrest of a human couple, murmuring in their sleep. These guardians haunt us because we are their kindred spirits, for we do not know where we are, since who we are "is too much to believe." We are "too sudden to be credible," and so the accurate image for us is "an inner haze," full kindred to mist and smoke. For all the genial tone, the spirit of "A Cabin in the Clearing" is negative even for Frost. His final letter, dictated just before his death, states an unanswerable question as though it were not a question: "How can we be just in a world that needs mercy and merciful in a world that needs justice." The Demiurge's laugh lurks behind the sentence, though Frost was then in no frame of spirit to indulge a demiurgic imagination.

Frost would have been well content to give his mentor Emerson the last word, though "content" is necessarily an inadequate word in this dark context. Each time I reread the magnificent essay, "Illusions," which concludes and crowns *The Conduct of Life*, I am reminded of the poetry of Robert Frost. The reminder is strongest in two paragraphs near the end that seem to be "Directive" writ large, as though Emerson had been brooding upon his descendant:

> We cannot write the order of the variable winds. How can we penetrate the law of our shifting moods and susceptibility? Yet they differ as all and nothing. Instead of the firmament of yesterday, which our eyes require, it is to-day an eggshell which coops us in; we cannot even see what or where our stars of destiny are. From day to day, the capital facts of human life are hidden from our eyes. Suddenly the mist rolls up, and reveals them, and we think how much good time is gone, that might have been saved, had any hint of these things been shown. A sudden rise in the road shows us the system of mountains, and all the summits, which have been just as near us all the year, but quite out of mind. But these alternations are not without their order, and we are parties to our various fortune. If life seem a

succession of dreams, yet poetic justice is done in dreams also. The visions of good men are good; it is the undisciplined will that is whipped with bad thoughts and bad fortunes. When we break the laws, we lose our hold on the central reality. Like sick men in hospitals, we change only from bed to bed, from one folly to another; and it cannot signify much what becomes of such castaways,—wailing, stupid, comatose creatures,—lifted from bed to bed, from the nothing of life to the nothing of death.

In this kingdom of illusions we grope eagerly for stays and foundations. There is none but a strict and faithful dealing at home, and a severe barring out of all duplicity or illusion there. Whatever games are played with us, we must play no games with ourselves, but deal in our privacy with the last honesty and truth. I look upon the simple and childish virtues of veracity and honesty as the root of all that is sublime in character. Speak as you think, be what you are, pay your debts of all kinds. I prefer to be owned as sound and solvent, and my word as good as my bond, and to be what cannot be skipped, or dissipated, or undermined, to all the *éclat* in the universe. This reality is the foundation of friendship, religion, poetry, and art. At the top or at the bottom of all illusions, I set the cheat which still leads us to work and live for appearances, in spite of our conviction, in all sane hours, that it is what we really are that avails with friends, with strangers, and with fate or fortune.

ROBERT PACK

Frost's Enigmatical Reserve:
The Poet as Teacher and Preacher

*I proposed to give one [course] in philosophy on judgments in
History, Literature, and Religion—how they are made and how they
stand, and I was taken on by the department [at Amherst] like odds
of a thousand to one. Well the debacle has begun. Here begins what
probably won't end till you see me in the pulpit.*

ROBERT FROST

In describing one of his own poems, Robert Frost says that it has the
"proper enigmatical reserve." Frost believed that the surface of a poem, like
speech, should be simple and immediate, yet that, upon further scrutiny,
the poem should reveal itself as elusive. After all, life does not readily yield
up its meaning and purpose—indeed, if it has any. The poet must be accurate
in describing his limited sense of the mysteries of nature and of God, and
he must be true to his own "confusion"—to use one of Frost's favorite
words. What the poem contains is not merely private knowledge but the
poet's own uncertainty, and the order the poem imposes on this uncertainty
functions to dramatize, not simplify or dismiss, what it is that puzzles him.
Frost said, "I don't like obscurity or obfuscation, but I do like dark sayings
I must leave the clearing of to time." If Frost as poet is also to be thought
of as teacher and preacher, then we, as readers, must regard his poems as
if they are parables. His poems speak most profoundly when they speak by
indirection; they are indeed "dark sayings," engagingly "enigmatical," and
the best of them maintain Frost's characteristic "reserve."

From *Affirming Limits: Essays on Mortality, Choice, and Poetic Form.* ©1985 by
The University of Massachusetts Press.

9

The dark qualities of a Frost poem, however, do not necessarily determine that the poem will be without humor. There is often an element of playfulness even in Frost's most serious poems. The play of the poem—the poet's power to create a design—is what Frost summons to contend with darkness and confusion. He takes delight in the resistance to uncertainty and disorder that humor can provide. About "The Road Not Taken," Frost said, "it's a tricky poem, very tricky." Frost had his own games to play with the game life demanded that he play:

> Forgive, O Lord, my little jokes on Thee
> And I'll forgive Thy great big one on me.

Frost's poems, then, are "tricky" out of a mischievous sense of delight in the intricacies of tone and image that a poem can organize, and "tricky," too, in that they themselves resemble the dangerous paths toward possible forgiveness and salvation that people must choose to follow in the course of their days. The image of the road appears in many poems, but it is always uncertain as to what revelation the road leads to, even when the destination or place is as specific as the "frozen wood" in "The Wood-Pile" or the old couple's new home in "In the Home Stretch."

Frost begins "The Oven Bird" with a playful and strategic lie: "There is a singer everyone has heard," he says. A reader, unaccustomed to Frostian trickery, will simply accept this line for what it states, but Frost knows perfectly well that not every reader has heard the call of an oven bird. And certainly no one has heard an oven bird that says "leaves are old" or "the early petal-fall is past" as he does in this poem:

> There is a singer everyone has heard,
> Loud, a mid-summer and a mid-wood bird,
> Who makes the solid tree trunks sound again.
> He says that leaves are old and that for flowers
> Mid-summer is to spring as one to ten.
> He says the early petal-fall is past
> When pear and cherry bloom went down in showers
> And comes that other fall we name the fall.
> He says the highway dust is over all.
> On sunny days a moment overcast;
> The bird would cease and be as other birds
> But that he knows in singing not to sing.
> The question that he frames in all but words
> Is what to make of a diminished thing.

Frost is playing a game with the reader's credulity, for the question of what we can believe on the basis of the little that we know is precisely the problem Frost is exploring here. What Frost is leading the reader toward is the contemplation of the design of the poem itself. Although the literal sound the bird makes is described merely as "loud" and is, in this sense, distracting, Frost invites the reader with him to "make" of this sound some speech that is humanly useful. Nature only speaks when man makes it speak. What man believes, beyond what he hears and sees, is necessarily of his own invention.

The oven bird's milieu is "mid-summer" and "mid-wood," yet the bird speaks of the "highway dust." Both man and bird, as it were, are midway in the journey of their lives, and though this road inevitably leads to dust and death, what matters most is the kind of song that man freely chooses to sing along the way. As Emerson says, "In popular experience everything good is on the highway." (Frost commented about Emerson, "I owe more to Emerson than anyone else for troubled thoughts about freedom.") The poet, lying his way hopefully toward the truth, tells us the bird "makes the solid tree trunks sound again." This new sound becomes the sound of the poet's voice incorporating and extending the literal call of the oven bird, just as Frost describes Eve in the garden of Eden listening to birds: she "added to their own an oversound." This addition is the result of human making, the invention of metaphor. Metaphor is fabrication, a lie the poet builds in the name of the truth, and thus it contains the reality of what the poet adds to what is there. Yet this making, enigmatic and uncertain, remains the only source of human belief. Such making is what Frost calls "real art ...believing the thing into existence, saying as you go more than you even hoped you were going to be able to say."

The season of fall is linked in "The Oven Bird" with the fall from the garden of Eden by the poetic act of naming: "And comes that other fall we name the fall." The poet has merged his voice with the oven bird, as Adam, in the book of Genesis, names the animals. So, too, the linking of literal meanings, speech, with poetic meanings, song, accomplishes the design by which the total poem exists in its own form and its own right. It is both sung prose and spoken song that enables Frost—as an oven bird—to know "in singing not to sing," for as speech can become song, and song can incorporate speech (as it does in this poem), so, too, can fact become metaphor, and metaphor, fact. These are the linkings that constitute poetic truth.

Belief for Frost is always grounded in the questions out of which belief emerges. As the maker of belief, this is what Frost teaches and what the poet proclaims is the virtual effect of the bird's song, which in reality is Frost's poem: "The question that he [both Frost and the oven bird] frames in all but words." The question is framed, just as the form of the sonnet constitutes a structural frame, and thus the question *implies* more than the words themselves can literally ask. The question embodies the *feeling* of the enigma of what man can make of himself and of his world: "Remember that the sentence sound often says more than the words," Frost once asserted. It is only because (like the bird's song) the poem is framed, because it is a made thing, that the question it asks, and the answer of belief that it implies, can remain dynamically in tension. The poem remains open to the reader's own scrutiny. Such is the style of Frostian teaching.

The question asked by the oven bird is "what to make of a diminished thing." It comes at the end of the poem and thus it throws us back to the beginning, so that the poem makes a kind of circle. But the question, though specific enough, is also enigmatic: What "diminished thing"? Summer is a diminishing from spring, as the oven bird says, "as one to ten." Fall is a diminishing from summer. The fall from the garden of Eden is a mythical diminishing. Death, the highway "dust," is the diminishment of life. (What can one make of death?) The poem is a diminishing of the oven bird's loud call and its *possible* meanings. (All poetic form is made by choice and selection and is thus a diminishing of nature's plenitude.) Aging on the highway, Frost, too, is a diminishing thing. The poem itself, however, is the poet's only answer to these questions, for it is, indeed, what the poet has made. It is an order, a design to set against uncertainty, to set against "the fall" and against death. As Frost consoled, "When in doubt there is always form for us to go on with." And thus the reader is left with the enigma of what to make of the poem, a thing "diminished" into shape from the chaos of life. Frost offers us a man-made form, and it is for us to be strengthened by it as such, to find in its own framed coherence what Frost himself believed to be there, "a momentary stay against confusion." And those readers who actually have heard the call of an oven bird (or have looked it up in Roger Tory Peterson's *A Field Guide to the Birds*) will know that what the oven bird says is: "Teacher! Teacher!"

II

If the role of the poet-teacher is to make nature speak with a human voice, the role of the poet-preacher is to dramatize for the reader the mystery of divinity in the face of which belief must be given shape. In this role, too, one finds the characteristic Frostian reserve:

> There may be little or much beyond the grave,
> But the strong are saying nothing until they see.

Or, in a lighter mood:

> And I may return
> If dissatisfied
> With what I learn
> From having died.

But Frost must speak—he must bear witness to the enigma of God in nature and offer his reader the story of that confrontation.

Frost describes a solitary man in his poem, "The Most of It," who walks out to a "boulder-broken beach," repeatedly it seems, to wake a voice that would answer his cry.

> He thought he kept the universe alone;
> For all the voice in answer he could wake
> Was but the mocking echo of his own
> From some tree-hidden cliff across the lake.
> Some morning from the boulder-broken beach
> He would cry out on life, that what it wants
> Is not its own love back in copy speech,
> But counter-love, original response.
> And nothing ever came of what he cried
> Unless it was the embodiment that crashed
> In the cliff's talus on the other side,
> And then in the far distant water splashed,
> But after a time allowed for it to swim,
> Instead of proving human when it neared
> And someone else additional to him,
> As a great buck it powerfully appeared,
> Pushing the crumpled water up ahead,
> And landed pouring like a waterfall,
> And stumbled through the rocks with horny tread,
> And forced the underbrush—and that was all.

The solitary man in the poem cries out as if to a god, unheeding or asleep, who might respond to his call if properly summoned. In his naive wish, he is like the boy of Winander in Wordsworth's *Prelude*, who "both hands /

Pressed closely palm to palm," as if in unconscious prayer, "Blew mimic hootings to the silent owls, / That they might answer him." But, unlike Frost's man, Wordsworth's boy does receive a certain answer, and he does hear a voice speaking in the silence. The owls "shout again / Responsive to his call." What Frost's man receives is merely the "mocking echo of his own" voice, and so the narrator tells us "He thought he kept the universe alone." The man is literally alone, and alone in the deeper sense that he is without a god who is the keeper, the protector, of the universe. A man may keep promises, but the universe is more than a man alone can keep or protect, more than he can keep watch over.

What the man cries out for, like Adam before the creation of Eve, is "counter-love, original response." He wishes for God's love, counter to man's need, and God's original creative presence. Without God, man's world is only a "boulder-broken beach," and man's voice calling out "on life" is a mockery of man's deepest desires. The narrator tells us that

> nothing ever came of what he cried
> Unless it was the embodiment that crashed
> In the cliff 's talus.

The whole mystery of this poem hangs on the open word "unless," on what the man (and the reader) makes of that crashing embodiment. The poem's enigma is whether to regard that embodiment as a kind of incarnation or revelation, or merely as a physical phenomenon that has occurred "some morning" by chance. If it is seen as an incarnation of God's design, then it is, indeed, the "most of it," the most the man can wish for: it is revelation. If it is merely a physical event and not God's "voice in answer," it must be seen as the limiting "most" man can receive from nature. The design of nature, then, would be no more than the design of nature alien to man.

The narrator describes the effect of the crashing embodiment literally, yet the impression the reader receives is uncertain and mysterious. There is a series of echoes. First, we hear the crash of loosening and tumbling stone. Then we hear the boulders splashing in the water. But what follows is a strange gap after which the boulders in the water *seem* to turn into a "great buck." The narrator says that this happens "after a time," as if it might be evolutionary time, as if the man has witnessed divine causality unfolding in a visionary instant. The narrator's difficult syntax suggests that it was the embodiment that allowed this transformation to take place. But even as the buck appears, it does not fulfill the man's expectation or hope. The buck is not seen as "original response," as "someone else additional to him." Like Adam naming the animals before the creation of Eve, the man senses that something is still missing in his world that has not yet been revealed. Described by the increasing elusive word "it," the buck is not regarded as the "most of it," although its natural power, like that of a waterfall, is awesome. The question still remains: Has the man witnessed more than a display of natural power?

What are the man, the narrator, the reader, to believe? The buck, with bountiful energy, "Pushing the crumpled water up ahead," seems to know what it is doing there, to have direction. But is this nature's random energy and force that "stumbled through the rocks," or is there the suggestion of a design that is to be read symbolically, as if life is to be seen here emerging from chaos and inorganic matter, pushing, landing, stumbling, forcing? The way the buck "forced the underbrush" resembles the way the image of the buck enters the mind of the man who is watching. That a powerful image is perceived is certain, but what can the mind make of that image, uniting rational thought with subconscious implications? It is as if the buck gets born in the mind of its perceiver. The narrator draws no conclusions, makes no assertions, and says flatly "that was all." Just as the title of the poem is firmly ambiguous in that "most" might mean everything the man hopes for, revelation, or merely the limit of what nature offers, so, too, is the last word, "all," ambiguous in the same way. Another voice echo occurs, "all" becomes an echo of "most." The phrase "that was all," therefore, with Frostian tonal irony, may imply disappointment, in that the man, hoping for a "voice in answer," sees only a buck, or "that was all" may suggest the man's jubilation in witnessing a gesture of divine revelation—all, everything. The buck, though not what the man expected, may be regarded as an embodiment of God's presence in nature—an embodiment that at least for Adam led to the creation of Eve. The poem keeps these alternative possibilities clearly and absolutely in balance. The readers, like the man in the poem, are left to believe, if they will, one or the other, or perhaps, more accurately, they are left, knowing the extremes of possibility—belief or disbelief—unable to choose, confirmed only in their uncertainty.

III

Can one become "whole again beyond confusion"? We see Frost again and again in his poems walking out into the darkness or venturing into an equivalent interior darkness, "To scare myself with my own desert places." Frost's intellectual heroism is his refusal to avoid such confrontation or to escape into comforting dogma. In his sonnet "Acquainted with the Night,"

written in Dantean terza rima, Frost is in his own circle of hell, locked into
an obsessive "I" of self-consciousness:

> I have been one acquainted with the night.
> I have walked out in rain—and back in rain.
> I have outwalked the furthest city light.
>
> I have looked down the saddest city lane.
> I have passed by the watchman on his beat
> And dropped my eyes, unwilling to explain.
>
> I have stood still and stopped the sound of feet
> When far away an interrupted cry
> Came over houses from another street,
>
> But not to call me back or say good-by;
> And further still at an unearthly height
> One luminary clock against the sky
>
> Proclaimed the time was neither wrong nor right.
> I have been one acquainted with the night.

The poem returns at the end to the line with which it begins, for there seems
to be no way out of this circle. The speaker's movements outward in body
and inward in thought both lead to the same darkness, the same "night."
The "city light," and later the moon, the "luminary clock," paradoxically
illuminate only this essential darkness, this absence of meaningful self-iden-
tity. We see the isolated speaker as if he were trying to walk beyond life
itself to confront death, the ultimate isolation. In doing so, he detaches
himself from the sorrow of human affairs as he looks back at the "saddest
city lane," and feels a pang of guilt as he passes "the watchman on his beat"
for the extreme alienation he has perversely chosen. And so he drops his
eyes, "unwilling to explain," even if he could, for he knows that the watchman is there to guard human lives and protect against the darkness, while
he has elected to submerge himself in it.

How much death, how much isolation, can one experience and still
return to tell of it? When the speaker says, "I have stood still and stopped
the sound of feet," the reader may feel that the speaker's heart has virtually
stopped, or worse, that his spirit has died within his stilled body. That this
is indeed spiritual death is suggested by the speaker's reaction to the anonymous "cry" that comes from the city of human suffering: the cry, he feels,
has nothing to do with him, it does "not call me back or say good-by."
Having "outwalked the furthest city light," the speaker, in his imagination,

journeys "further still," even beyond the world, to an "unearthly height," and envisions the moon as a clock. But time, the cosmos itself, is regarded as being without moral content and thus without meaning: it is "neither wrong nor right." To feel this way, in effect, is to be in hell. Such is the dark night that Frost confronts and finds within himself.

But the speaker does return, just as the poem returns to its first line. Close to death as he has come, he has not died and experienced the ultimate isolation, nor has he wrung from death its mystery. He says, having said it before, "I have been one acquainted with the night," and the reader knows that he has been, is, and will continue to be so acquainted. He will go on. He will, for a time, outwalk the death within him. He is "one"—he feels himself to be alone—but such confining isolation is not equal to death itself. He still does not *know* death, for he is merely "*acquainted* with the night." This is what he comes back to tell us. As far as we may journey into darkness, we can never know the final darkness or discover what ultimately it may reveal. All we can know is that we are lost. With this paradoxical knowledge, we may begin our journey again, and if we are "lost enough to find [ourselves]," we will go on trying to assert form—such as the circle this poem strategically makes—where there is darkness.

What every Frostian confrontation with nature teaches is that God's ways and his purpose for men are obscure, and the poet, the preacher, must lead the reader to prayer without denying or sentimentalizing the divine mystery. Frost's courage is to live within the circle of doubt and yet still to try to approach God through prayer. But as he says, "People should be careful how they pray. I've seen about as much harm as good come from prayer. It is highly doubtful if man is equipped for judicious prayer." The paradox of "judicious prayer" is that it is not the result of reason, but of belief, and belief, for Frost, is always an invention. Frost, in the voice of God speaking to Job, says in *A Masque of Reason*, "There's no connection man can reason out / Between his just deserts and what he gets." Frost must be the inventor of prayer, guiding his reader, in the hope that the human drive toward making form and order corresponds to something like a divine command to do so. And yet human order, the poem, must always acknowledge that in nature itself God's meaning is not to be discerned. The poet-preacher must teach his readers to pray that they be able to pray; he must teach them the absolute humility—that man is not capable of judging his own works or his own worth. If there is a divine mercy, perhaps it is God's response to such humility, or as Frost says in *A Masque of Mercy*:

Our lives laid down in war and peace, may not
Be found acceptable in Heaven's sight.
And that they may be is the only prayer
Worth praying.

IV

In "The Draft Horse," an anonymous couple, like Adam and Eve late in the world's history, are seen on a typically unspecified journey:

With a lantern that wouldn't burn
In too frail a buggy we drove
Behind too heavy a horse
Through a pitch-dark limitless grove.

And a man came out of the trees
And took our horse by the head
And reaching back to his ribs
Deliberately stabbed him dead.

The ponderous beast went down
With a crack of a broken shaft.
And the night drew through the trees
In one long invidious draft.

The most unquestioning pair
That ever accepted fate
And the least disposed to ascribe
Any more than we had to to hate,

We assumed that the man himself
Or someone he had to obey
Wanted us to get down
And walk the rest of the way.

We do not know whether this couple are leaving home or returning home. They are in "too frail a buggy," suggesting the frailty of their bodies, and their lantern, suggesting their reason, sheds no light. It is "pitch dark," nothing can be seen. The narrative of the poem is enacted in this total darkness, so that, in effect, everything that takes place is imagined as in a nightmare vision. The grove through which the couple move is "limitless." It would seem that there can be no end to their journey, no destination that might reveal the purpose and meaning of their travel's effort. The thought of infinitude is itself a tormenting part of their dilemma. Suddenly, a figure, described blankly as "a man," comes out of the woods and stabs their horse dead. His action is assumed to be deliberate, but for what intent and purpose, we do not know. Since the act occurs in absolute darkness, the reader can only assume that the speaker of the poem *assumes* that it is a man. It might as well be an angel or a devil or the speaker's own guilty fantasy. And the assumption that this is a deliberate act is also enigmatic: Has the man done this out of evil, merely to harm, or is there some purpose in the act, since it forces the couple to dismount and make their way through the dark entirely by the strength of their own spirits?

Having first been described as "too heavy a horse," the "beast" goes down "ponderous" with the weight of its own mortality. Everything weighs finally what death weighs. Death determines the measure of all things, and the "shaft," which seemingly gave the horse direction and purpose, is broken. If the "little horse" in "Stopping by Woods on a Snowy Evening" shows an instinct to return home, not to remain in the dangerously enticing woods, the heavy horse in this poem reveals only that this basic wish may be defeated. And just as the mysterious man has come "out of the trees," so, too, does the night move "through the trees" as if the man and the night were the same or were directed by the same force. The night moves in an "invidious draft," enwrapping and destroying the "draft horse"; their names merge, agent and victim become one, and all is reduced to a wind. The work of the draft horse has been completed, but nothing that the poem's speaker can understand through reason has been accomplished.

Can anything be made of this apparently meaningless and random event? The speaker describes himself and his companion as an "unquestioning pair." They are not, however, unthinking; they seem to know that knowledge has its limits in this "limitless grove," and, quite simply, they must accept this. They accept "fate" as a necessity, knowing that their freedom, if it exists at all, exists only in the attitude they take toward their fate, and thus the speaker says that they are "the least disposed to ascribe / Any more than we had to to hate." In their reluctance to respond to this event as the design of a malevolent force (a "design of darkness to appall"), they begin to define their own humanity. They will have to make something positive from this seemingly rebuking event—something that derives from their own humanity, though they will never be certain that they are right to attribute this generosity to anything other than themselves. They will have only the fragile certainty of what belief provides. And yet the believer may speculate that this is precisely what God wants, precisely what his design demands: that we must respond to nature, and thus to God, out of our own believing, not God's revelation. Therein lies our freedom. In this sense, it is the meaning that we make out of unmeaning that reveals us in our greatest humanity. God says to Job in *A Masque of Reason*:

> Too long I've owed you this apology
> For the apparently unmeaning sorrow
> You were afflicted with in those old days.
> But it was of the essence of the trial
> You shouldn't understand it at the time.
> It had to seem unmeaning to have meaning.

The ability to make meaning of "apparently unmeaning sorrow" is synonymous with our ability to pray. We must not pray *for* something; rather, we must *make* something and hope the trial of that uncertain making will lead to our salvation, if not beyond the grave, at least within the measure of time.

And so, in "The Draft Horse," the couple make what may be called a creative *assumption*. They choose to accept the apparently causeless punishment of fate as having a positive aspect. They assume that nature and human events must "obey" the laws of fate and that there is intent behind this design that must remain obscure to them. The man—that mysterious agent—no less than themselves, obeys the author of this design. The grove, the night, the wind, the man, the journeying couple—all are part of the design. And the only free act that the couple can perform is to "assume" that there is meaning in this enigmatical design. The closest Frost comes to naming God in this poem is when he refers to "someone [the man] had to obey," yet an unknowable God is there by implication. What this obscure, controlling force demands, or so the couple choose to assume, is only that they "get down / And walk the rest of the way." Why this "someone" wants this, they are not told, and they do not know. Just as the grove is limitless, so, too, are the possible explanations for what the couple have experienced and what the reader has been given to witness. Although reason cannot unravel the mystery of what is limitless, Frost's parable is rich with implications that he, as poet-preacher, has locked into the poem with firm intent. The poem itself resists the darkness that it confronts, both as a man-made order and as an assumption that the outer darkness, the cosmos, is also an order, and, as such, may be believed to contain a benevolent intent. This is the inherent prayer the poem makes and invites the reader to participate in. And so to this darkness the poet-teacher must unceasingly turn, for it is the source of all that he is and all that he may become, as Frost said in his letter to "The Amherst Student":

The background [is] hugeness and confusion shading away from where we stand into black and utter chaos; and against the background any small man-made figure of order and concentration. What pleasanter than that it should be so? . . . This confusion . . . we like it, we were born to it, used to it and have practical reasons for wanting it there. To me any little form I assert upon it is velvet, as the saying is, and to be considered for how much more it is than nothing.

(Selected Prose of Robert Frost)

Perhaps, then, the readers themselves may assume that there is indeed good in the couple's having to "walk the rest of the way," entirely on their own. They are compelled to make of "the way" what they can and what they will, just as the poet has made the finite form of his poem out of unlimited darkness. Where the "way" will lead, the poem does not tell us, but as Frost says, "The one inalienable right is to go to destruction in your own way. What's worth living for is worth dying for." What lies beyond the grave the strong do not venture to guess at. There may be nothing, and that enigma remains part of the darkness in which we live. But if Frost as teacher, preacher, and poet, "acquainted with the night," is to keep going along the way, and if he is to be true to the God he believes in but does not know, he must imitate his enigmatical creator and maintain his own "proper enigmatical reserve" in the making of his poems.

FRANK LENTRICCHIA

The Redemptive Imagination

there are no two things as important in life and art as being
threatened and being saved. What are ideals of form for if we
aren't going to be made to fear for them? All our ingenuity is
lavished on getting into danger legitimately so that we may be
genuinely rescued.

ROBERT FROST in a letter, 7 June 1937

The relation of art to life is of the first importance especially
in a skeptical age since, in the absence of a belief in God, the
mind turns to its own creations and examines them, not alone
from the aesthetic point of view, but for what they reveal, for
what they validate and invalidate, for the support that they
give.

WALLACE STEVENS, *Adagia*

In recent years a compelling and cogent argument for the skepticism of
the great English romantics has been made by Harold Bloom, Geoffrey
Hartman, David Perkins, David Ferry, and others. Directed with considerable polemical force (particularly by Bloom) at the antiromanticism of
the New Critics and their followers, this argument has convincingly made
Wordsworth and company charter members of the modern literary community. It is not possible, now, not to see the romantics as fathers of
modernist poetry; not possible, now, to read them as noumenally naive
believers in the healing powers of imagination. But the case for skepticism
has been much overstated, as perhaps it had to be, and some ineradicable
(and crucial) discontinuities in literary history since Wordsworth have been
blurred. A stubborn and strange refusal by recent romantic critics to acknowledge basic differences in the philosophical contexts of the early ʳ

From *Robert Frost: Modern Poetics and the Landscapes of Self.* ©1975 by Duke
University Press.

23

mantics and certain twentieth-century writers has led to the postulation of
more continuity in the literary history of the past century and a half than
in fact exists. It is of course true that the malaise of self-consciousness—a
central point of comparison—has its origins in the romantic movement, and
true that modern writers wrestle the problem. But it is also true that our
modern writers tend to have an even more minimal vision of human community and the community of man and nature than do the early romantics.
A stricter accounting for the immense impact of naturalism (and for various
other philosophical movements that contributed to the "disappearance of
God") might be sobering for the devotees of romantic continuities.

Neither Robert Frost nor Wallace Stevens, for example, feels a hatred
for the "limits of mortality"—to borrow the title of David Ferry's book on
Wordsworth—because neither Frost nor Stevens has in their cultural contexts a paradigm and a *promise* (however difficult to realize) for the ultimate
romantic cure of alienation, the metaphysical continuity of subject and
object which breaks down the prison of subjectivity. For Frost the redemption of alienation is never an experience of metaphysical transcendence, as
it sometimes is in Wordsworth. For Frost the frequent failure to redeem
alienation is never accompanied (as it sometimes is in Wordsworth) by the
sense that human limitation has cruelly denied him the experience of what
he believes to be most profoundly true of human beings and their relationship to the natural world. If we wish to seek typological parallels for Frost
and Wordsworth we would look to Nietzsche and Schelling respectively.
And an awareness of the chasm that separates these two philosophers may
help us to keep separated the varieties of romanticism.

The concept of a secularly generated "redemption," with its locus
within the moment of aesthetic imagining, is not an invention of Wallace
Stevens (despite rumors to the contrary), but a fundamental postulate of
romantic tradition. In the romantic formulation the concept is deeply psychological, not theological. The model, though, is the Redeemer of the
Biblical story and His relationship to the creation. In the romantic and
postromantic transformation, the redemptive force gets transferred to imaginative consciousness; it is a kind of creative perception, and the key relationship becomes the epistemological one of subject (as redeemer) and object
(as that-to-be-redeemed). What most distinguishes Frost from earlier apocalyptic romantics—who are often painfully aware of the disjunction of
nature and consciousness—is his guarded awareness that redemptive consciousness is only human, all too human. The consolations of imagination
are at best modest and they tend to be limited to aesthetic illusion. From

the traditional perspective this is meager, perhaps even meaningless stuff. But our best twentieth-century poets refuse to claim more.

Redemptive consciousness is reflected in Frost in the merging of self with another ("The Pasture," "Going for Water"); in the merging of lovers with history which is grasped, in their love, as a continuous whole ("The Generations of Men"); in the merging of self with nature ("Rose Pogonias," "The Quest of the Purple-Fringed"); in the merging of self with the workaday world (as that world is transformed by the self's play energies in a poem like "The Mountain"); in the serenity of self within an imagined world, an enclosure which fences out actuality ("The Black Cottage," "The Census Taker"); and, finally, because of any or all of these resolutions, redemptive consciousness is reflected in the resolution of inner tensions as the self comes into harmony with itself, feeling relief that passes all understanding.

Three qualifications need to be made. First, the moment of redemptive vision in Frost is only, usually, a moment. With few exceptions it tends to be hedged in by skeptical, ironic consciousness. (The last lines of "Two Look at Two" are a splendid example of this complexity.) And in an ironic consciousness, separateness, finitude, and tensions plague the self once more. Second, the resolutions which occur in Frost occur wholly within imaginative awareness, and this emphasizes the purely phenomenological validity of those redemptive moments. Frost claims neither explicitly nor implicitly that his resolutions have a metaphysical correspondence in the nature of things, nor that they can work for anyone else. Though such redemptions and their ramifications are wholly psychological and personal, they are not any less valuable for Robert Frost. Third, redemptions need not result always in therapeutic experiences, because they are often projected out of countertherapeutic acts of consciousness.

I

The mass of men lead lives of quiet desperation. . . . There is no play in them, for this comes after work.

—THOREAU

"Mending Wall" is the opening poem of Frost's second volume, *North of Boston*. One of the dominating moods of this volume, forcefully established in such important poems as "The Death of the Hired Man," "Home Burial," "The Black Cottage," and "A Servant to Servants," and carried through some of the minor pieces, flows from the tension of having to maintain balance at the precipitous edge of hysteria. With "The Mountain" and with "A Hundred Collars," "Mending Wall" stands opposed to such visions of human existence; more precisely put, to existences that are fashioned by the neurotic visions of central characters like the wife in "Home Burial," the servant in "A Servant to Servants." "Mending Wall" dramatizes the redemptive imagination in its playful phase, guided surely and confidently by a man who has his world under full control, who in his serenity is riding his realities, not being shocked by them into traumatic response. The place of "Mending Wall" in the structure of *North of Boston* suggests, in its sharp contrasts to the dark tones of some of the major poems in the volume, the psychological necessities of sustaining supreme fictions.

The opening lines evoke the coy posture of the shrewd imaginative man who understands the words of the farmer in "The Mountain": "All the fun's in how you say a thing."

> Something there is that doesn't love a wall,
> That sends a frozen-ground-swell under it
> And spills the upper boulders in the sun,
> And makes gaps even two can pass abreast.

It does not take more than one reading of the poem to understand that the speaker is not a country primitive who is easily spooked by the normal processes of nature. He knows very well what it is "that doesn't love a wall" (frost, of course). His fun lies in not naming it. And in not naming the scientific truth he is able to manipulate intransigent fact into the world of the mind where all things are pliable. The artful vagueness of the phrase "Something there is" is enchanting and magical, suggesting even the hushed tones of reverence before mystery in nature. And the speaker (who is not at all reverent toward nature) consciously works at deepening that sense of mystery:

> The work of hunters is another thing:
> I have come after them and made repair
> Where they have left not one stone on a stone,
> But they would have the rabbit out of hiding,
> To please the yelping dogs. The gaps I mean,
> No one has seen them made or heard them made,
> But at spring mending-time we find them there.

The play of the mature, imaginative man is grounded in ironic awareness—and must be. Even as he excludes verifiable realities from his fictive world the unmistakable tone of scorn for the hunters comes seeping through. He may step into a fictive world but not before glancing back briefly at the brutality that attends upon the play of others. Having paid for his imaginative excursions by establishing his complex awareness, he is free to close the magic circle cast out by his playful energies, and close out the world reported by the senses ("No one has seen them made or heard them made"). In knowing how to say a thing in and through adroit linguistic manipulation, the fiction of the "something" that doesn't love a wall is created; the imagined reality stands formed before him, ready to be entered.

Like the selves dramatized in "Going for Water" and "The Tuft of Flowers," this persona would prefer not to be alone in his imaginative journey:

> I let my neighbor know beyond the hill;
> And on a day we meet to walk the line
> And set the wall between us once again.
> We keep the wall between us as we go.
> To each the boulders that have fallen to each.
> And some are loaves and some so nearly balls
> We have to use a spell to make them balance:
> "Stay where you are until our backs are turned!"
> We wear our fingers rough with handling them.
> Oh, just another kind of outdoor game,
> One on a side. It comes to little more:
> There where it is we do not need the wall:
> He is all pine and I am apple orchard.
> My apple trees will never get across
> And eat the cones under his pines, I tell him.
> He only says, "Good fences make good neighbors."

If the fact of a broken wall is excuse enough to make a fiction about why it got that way, then that same fact may be the occasion for two together to take a journey in the mind. For those still tempted to read "Mending Wall" as political allegory (the narrator standing for a broad-minded liberal internationalism, the thick-headed second speaker representing a selfish super-patriot) they must first face the line "I let my neighbor know beyond the hill." "Mending Wall" has nothing to do with one-world political ideals, with good or bad neighbor policies: on this point the title of the poem is helpful. It is a poem that celebrates a process, not the thing itself. It is a poem, furthermore, that distinguishes between two kinds of people: one who seizes the particular occasion of mending as fuel for the imagination and as a release from the dull ritual of work each spring and one who is trapped by work and by the New England past as it comes down to him in the form of his father's cliché. Tied as he is to his father's words that "Good fences make good neighbors," the neighbor beyond the hill is committed to an end, the fence's completion. His participation in the process of rebuilding is sheer work—he never plays the outdoor game. The narrator, however, is not committed to ends, but to the process itself which he sees as having nonutilitarian value: "There where it is we do not need the wall." The process itself is the matrix of the play that redeems work by transforming it into the pleasure of an outdoor game in which you need to cast spells to make rocks balance. Overt magic-making is acceptable in the world of this poem because we are governed by the narrator's perspective; we are in the fictive world where all things are possible, where walls go tumbling for mysterious reasons. Kant's theory that work and the aesthetic activity are antagonistic, polar activities of man is, in effect, disproven, as the narrator makes work take on the aesthetic dimension. The real differences between the two people in the poem is that one moves in a world of freedom; aware of the resources of the mind, he nurtures the latent imaginative power within himself and makes it a factor in everyday living; while the other, unaware of the value of imagination, must live his unliberated life without it. And this difference makes a difference in the quality of the life lived.

The narrator of "Mending Wall" does not give up easily: he tries again to tempt his neighbor to enter into the fictive world with him and to share his experience of play:

> Spring is the mischief in me, and I wonder
> If I could put a notion in his head:
> "*Why* do they make good neighbors? Isn't it
> Where there are cows? But here there are no cows.
> Before I built a wall I'd ask to know
> What I was walling in or walling out,
> And to whom I was like to give offense.
> Something there is that doesn't love a wall,
> That wants it down." I could say "Elves" to him,
> But it's not elves exactly, and I'd rather
> He said it for himself.

All to no avail: the outrageously appropriate pun on "offense"—a linguistic emblem of the poem's spirit of play and freedom—falls on deaf ears. The neighbor won't say "elves," those little folk who don't love a wall; he will not enter the play world of imagination. He moves in "darkness," our narrator concludes, "like an old-stone savage armed." The characterization is philosophically precise in the logic of post-Kantian aesthetics; the recalcitrant and plodding neighbor is a slave to the rituals of the quotidian, a primitive whose spirit has not been freed by the artistic consciousness that lies dormant within. It is the play spirit of imagination, as Schiller suggests, which distinguishes the civilized man from his cave-dwelling ancestor—that "old stone-savage" who moved in "darkness."

II

In "Birches" (*Mountain Interval*, 1916) Frost begins to probe the power of his redemptive imagination as it moves from its playful phase toward the brink of dangerous transcendence. The movement into transcendence is a movement into a realm of radical imaginative freedom where (because redemption has succeeded too well) all possibilities of engagement with the common realities of experience are dissolved. In its moderation, a redemptive consciousness motivates union between selves as we have seen [previously] in "The Generations of Men," or in any number of Frost's love poems. But in its extreme forms, redemptive consciousness can become self-defeating as it presses the imaginative man into deepest isolation.

"Birches" begins by evoking its core image against the background of a darkly wooded landscape:

> When I see birches to left and right
> Across the lines of straighter darker trees,
> I like to think some boy's been swinging them.
> But swinging doesn't bend them down to stay
> As ice storms do.

The pliable, malleable quality of the birch tree captures the poet's attention and kicks off his meditation. Perhaps young boys don't bend birches down to stay, but swing them they do and thus bend them momentarily. Those "straighter, darker trees," like the trees of "Into My Own" that "scarcely show the breeze," stand ominously free from human manipulation, menacing in their irresponsiveness to acts of the will. The malleability of the birches is not total, however, and the poet is forced to admit this fact into the presence of his desire, like it or not. The ultimate shape of mature birch trees is the work of objective natural force, not human activity. Yet after

conceding the boundaries of imagination's subjective world, the poet seems
not to have constricted himself but to have been released.

> Often you must have seen them
> Loaded with ice a sunny winter morning
> After a rain. They click upon themselves
> As the breeze rises, and turn many-colored
> As the stir cracks and crazes their enamel.
> Soon the sun's warmth makes them shed crystal shells
> Shattering and avalanching on the snow crust—
> Such heaps of broken glass to sweep away
> You'd think the inner dome of heaven had fallen.

Fascinated as he is by the show of loveliness before him, and admir-
ing as he is of nature as it performs the potter's art, cracking and crazing
the enamel of ice coating on the birch trees, it is not finally the thing itself
(the ice-coated trees) that interests the poet but the strange association he
is tempted to make: "You'd think the inner dome of heaven had fallen."
Certainly there is no question of belief involved here. The linkage of the
scientifically discredited medieval sphere with the heaps of cracked ice
suggests rather the poet's need to break beyond the rigid standard of empirical truth, that he himself has already allowed into the poem, and
faintly suggests as well the kind of apocalyptic destruction that the imagination seeks when unleashed (the idea that the inner dome has been
smashed clearly pleases the speaker). Eventually Frost in "Birches" comes
round to exploring in much more sophisticated ways the complex problem broached by this statement from a later poem, "On Looking Up by
Chance at the Constellations":

> The sun and moon get crossed, but they never touch,
> Nor strike out fire from each other, nor crash out loud.
> The planets seem to interfere in their curves,
> But nothing ever happens, no harm is done.
> We may as well go patiently on with our life,
> And look elsewhere than to the stars and moon and sun
> For the shocks and changes we need to keep us sane.

In "Birches" Frost looks not to natural catastrophe for those "shocks
and changes" that "keep us sane" but to his resources as a poet:

You may see their trunks arching in the woods
Years afterwards, trailing their leaves on the ground
Like girls on hands and knees that throw their hair
Before them over their heads to dry in the sun.

Manipulating the simile, the overt figure of comparison, is a dangerous ploy for the poet, implying often that he does not have the courage of his vision and does not believe that his mode of language can generate a distinctive perspective on experience. For Frost, however, and for any poet who is rooted in what I call the aesthetics of the fiction, the simile is the perfect figure of comparison, subtler even than metaphor. Its overtness becomes its virtue: in its insistence on the disparateness of the things compared (as well as their likeness) it can sustain a divided vision; can at once transmute the birches—for a brief moment nature stands humanized and the poet has transcended the scientific universe—and, at the same time, can allow the fictive world to be penetrated by the impurities of experience that resist the transmutative process of imagination. It is at such moments as this in Frost's work that the strategies and motives of a poetry of play are revealed. There is never any intention of competing with science and, therefore, there is no problem at all (as we generally sense with many modern poets and critics) of claiming a special cognitive value for poetry. In his playful and redemptive mode, Frost's motive for poetry is not cognitive but psychological in the sense that he is willfully seeking to bathe his consciousness and, if the reader consents, his reader's as well, in a free-floating, epistemologically unsanctioned vision of the world which, even as it is undermined by the very language in which it is anchored, brings a satisfaction of relief when contemplated. It may be argued that the satisfaction is greatest when it is autonomous: the more firmly the poet insists upon the severance of his vision from the order of things as they are and the more clearly that he makes no claim for knowledge, the emotive power of the poem may emerge uncontaminated by the morass of philosophical problems that are bound to dog him should he make claims for knowledge. Both poet and reader may submerge themselves without regret (because without epistemological pretension) in aesthetic illusion.

But I was going to say when Truth broke in
With all her matter of fact about the ice storm,
I should prefer to have some boy bend them
As he went out and in to fetch the cows—
Some boy too far from town to learn baseball,

> Whose only play was what he found himself,
> Summer or winter, and could play alone.

The shrewdness in Frost's strategy now surfaces. While claiming to have paid homage to the rigid standards of empirical truth in his digression on the ice-loaded branches, what he has actually done is to digress into the language of fictions. When he turns to the desired vision of the young boy swinging birches, he is not, as he says, turning from truth to fiction, but from one kind of fiction to another kind of fiction: from the fiction of cosmic change and humanized nature to the fiction of the human will riding rough-shod over a pliable external world. And the motives for all of this fooling? I think there are two: one is that Frost intends to fox his naturalistically persuaded readers; a second is that this is what his poem is all about—the thrusting of little fictions within alien, antifictive contexts. As he evokes the image of the boy, playing in isolation, too far from the community to engage in a team kind of sport, he evokes, as well, his cherished theme of the imaginative man who, essentially alone in the world, either makes it or doesn't on the strength of his creative resources. And now he indulges to the full the desired vision that he could not allow himself in the poem's opening lines:

> One by one he subdued his father's trees
> By riding them down over and over again
> Until he took the stiffness out of them,
> And not one but hung limp, not one was left
> For him to conquer. He learned all there was
> To learn about not launching out too soon
> And so not carrying the tree away
> Clear to the ground. He always kept his poise
> To the top branches, climbing carefully
> With the same pains you use to fill a cup
> Up to the brim, and even above the brim.
> Then he flung outward, feet first, with a swish,
> Kicking his way down through the air to the ground.

One figure seems to imply another—the image of the farm youth swinging up, out, and down to earth again recalls the boyhood of the poet:

> So was I once myself a swinger of birches.
> And so I dream of going back to be.
> It's when I'm weary of considerations,

And life is too much like a pathless wood
Where your face burns and tickles with the cobwebs
Broken across it, and one eye is weeping
From a twig's having lashed across it open.

For anyone but Frost the "pathless wood" is trite. But for him it carries a complex of meaning fashioned elsewhere. The upward swinging of the boy becomes an emblem for imagination's swing away from the tangled, dark wood; a swing away from the "straighter, darker trees"; a swing into the absolute freedom of isolation, the severing of all "considerations." This is the transcendental phase of redemptive consciousness, a game that one plays alone. The downward movement of redemptive imagination to earth, contrarily, is a movement into community, engagement, love—the games that two play together:

I'd like to get away from earth awhile
And then come back to it and begin over.
May no fate willfully misunderstand me
And half grant what I wish and snatch me away
Not to return. Earth's the right place for love:
I don't know where it's likely to go better.
I'd like to go by climbing a birch tree,
And climb black branches up a snow-white trunk
Toward heaven, till the tree could bear no more,
But dipped its top and set me down again.
That would be good both going and coming back.
One could do worse than be a swinger of birches.

One really has no choice but to be a swinger of birches. In the moment when, catapulting upward, the poet is half-granted his wish, when transcendence is about to be complete and the self, in its disdain for earth, has lofted itself into absolute autonomy, nothing having any claim upon it, and no return possible, then, at that moment, the blessed pull of the earth is felt again, and the apocalypse desired by a transcending imagination, which seemed so imminent, is repressed. At the end of "Birches" a precious balance has been restored between the claims of a redeeming imagination in its extreme, transcendent form, and the claims of common sense reality. To put it another way, the psychic needs of change—supplied best by redemptive imagination—are balanced by the equally deep psychic need—supplied by skeptical ironic awareness—for the therapy of dull realities and everyday considerations.

III

In its difficult and dense linguistic configurations within which a complex network of meanings is embedded, in its rapid and radical shifts of
tone and attitude that evoke a wide range of responses, and in its masterful
blank verse rhythms that sustain his ultimate in lyrical expression, we are
pointed to one idea: that "Directive" is Frost's *summa*, his most compelling
and encompassing meditation on the possibilities of redemption through
the imagination, the one poem that a critic of Frost must sooner or later
confront if he hopes to grasp the poet's commitment to his art as a way of
saving himself, and to understand the astonishing unity of his life's work
at last fully revealed here in this major poem of his later career. The inter-
locking motifs and symbols from the earlier poems are there: the lonely
man out on an even lonelier journey, seeking to withdraw; the image of the
house now only a crumbling foundation overgrown with wild flowers; the
deliberate, self-conscious projecting of illusions; the image of the woods;
the overt references to play; the image of a vanishing human world; lastly,
the crucial reference to the brook. But "Directive" is no collection of old
stories: it does not represent the artist in his last phase of the great pretender,
reduced in his aesthetic poverty to imitating himself. The landscape established in many other poems emerges in "Directive," but it is fashioned anew,
the context is fresh.

In the poem's opening lines the narrator issues the first of several "directives" to his reader:

> Back out of all this now too much for us,
> Back in a time made simple by the loss
> Of detail, burned, dissolved, and broken off
> Like graveyard marble sculpture in the weather,
> There is a house that is no more a house
> Upon a farm that is no more a farm
> And in a town that is no more a town.

Possibly only the poet can risk issuing such directives which, because of
their ambiguous and even contradictory implications, lead not to action—
as the rhetorician's language is calculated to so prompt us—but to troubled
and bewildered contemplation. We must immediately acclimatize ourselves
to a context within which linguistic playfulness and the grimmest of issues
are the most compatible friends. The imperative tone in the opening lines
is lost if we do not recognize the play over the phrases "Back out of," "Back
in" which idiomatically refer us to time past—and in part that is what the
poet intends—but which literally command us to a certain kind of move-

ment. We are being asked to "back off," really, to withdraw from over-
whelming confusion. The image projected in these lines is of a man
overcome, warily withdrawing from the present with both eyes fixed on the
"now" that is "too much," as if it were a cunning enemy that you could
not for a moment turn your back on. It is painful but true that the value
of withdrawal rests on the continuing presence (at least in the mind) of that
which one no longer wants present: the rushing, unmanageable present itself
and a number of facts about the human condition that Frost will not let us
conceal from ourselves. His first directive is curious, finally, not only because
it is cast in the language of double talk but also because, unlike most
directives, it is issued not from above, from one who is situated outside of
the chaos that he orders us out of. "Now" is "too much for us"—the poet's
directive has self-reflexive force.

However strong the desire for withdrawal may be, we might finally
find ourselves frozen in our backward movement: what we are withdrawing
to seems hardly more promising than what we are withdrawing *from*. It is
difficult to feel nostalgic about the trip back through time when it gives all
the appearances of being a trip through decay and destruction, through
nature's morgue. Our journey through time promises to take us by mon-
uments of time's conflagration: things "burned," things "dissolved," things
"broken off." And when we finally make it to the desired simplicity of the
promised land, we will be rewarded with three images of desertion and
death: the house, the farm, and the town that are no more. At this point
the journey doesn't seem worth our trouble. I would venture the guess,
though, that the poet's intention is to make it as difficult as possible and
to warn us that it will be hard from the very outset. As he put it in "Mowing,"
he does not offer "easy gold at the hand of fay or elf." The "wrong ones,"
as he suggests in the concluding lines of "Directive," echoing St. Mark, will
be discouraged long before he can lead them to the treasures of a special
kind of redemption—they won't "get saved." He insists that those who do
get saved have an encompassing kind of consciousness that can entertain
and retain clashing values and visions. Frost's ideal man of imagination has
to be a tough and resilient type who can stay whole though he is pulled in
opposite directions by powerful forces, hung between a present that is con-
fusing and unliveable and a past that is littered with death's remains. He
has, apparently, nowhere to go, even as he withdraws.

The narrator continues, with qualification, in gentle tones not at all
typical of those who issue directives:

> The road there, if you'll let a guide direct you
> Who only has at heart your getting lost,

> May seem as if it should have been a quarry—
> Great monolithic knees the former town
> Long since gave up pretence of keeping covered.

The guide is the poet-narrator and the journey that he is asking us to take with him—if we should consent—is more than a long walk on one of Frost's long-closed New England roads that lead back, even today, to towns where nobody lives. We are taking with him a journey in the imagination, backing up the stream of time, and the lostness that he hopes we shall come to feel will be something different from a sense of spatial dislocation, with our compasses all out of order. We are, or so we hope, going to lose one kind of existence in order to gain a more valuable one.

The progress (and direction) of our steady withdrawal can be measured by the changes wrought by the forces of nature. Just below the busted road laid down by the men of the town long ago sits the imperturbable, eternal raw rock. Its cold and hard face again dominates the scene and the "pretence" of human control has been shattered, subverted from beneath, as it were. This image makes it clear that no salvation awaits us in the barren rock-ribbed hills; this is a setting that will not caress the bruised psyche. The narrator is inviting us, with ever so much tact, quietly destroying any last harbored romantic illusions about our relations to history and the external universe, but simultaneously introducing more modest illusions of his own, hoping now not to command us but to beguile, hoping to slip inside our defenses against the enchantments of a difficult trip.

> And there's a story in a book about it:
> Besides the wear of iron wagon wheels
> The ledges show lines ruled southeast-northwest,
> The chisel work of an enormous Glacier
> That braced his feet against the Arctic Pole.
> You must not mind a certain coolness from him
> Still said to haunt this side of Panther Mountain.
> Nor need you mind the serial ordeal
> Of being watched from forty cellar holes
> As if by eye pairs out of forty firkins.

Implicitly we are being invited to assume the magic of the poet's perspective in order to ease the burdens of a lonely journey. Geological history—and specifically that part of it belonging to the Ice Age—is casually mythologized. Historical record when seen as "a story in a book" takes on the quality of an imagined—a constructed—reality and its forbidding posture as intransigent fact is dissolved away in whimsical personification. A humanized nature, projected in this myth, however cool, is preferable to the thing really there beneath the myth. The lightness of Frost's touch in this passage, markedly contrasting to the tone of the poem's beginning, is meant to get us over a difficult place in the journey, to take us deeper with the least amount of pain. The comparison, purposely left submerged, is between the kind of force that it took to chisel a lasting mark on the stony face of nature—a force massive and beyond comprehension—and the embarrassingly puny and futile human effort, the pretence to keep those forbidding knees covered. Frost generally builds in an escape hatch: in this passage, if we should grasp the unstated comparison between nature and man, if we should then become disillusioned at the image of the human will given, why then there are the lines, alongside those made by the Glacier, worn in rock by our wagon wheels, years and years of wagon wheels, attesting to our tenacious stamina. We are not all that ephemeral, after all, unless, that is, we insist on scrutinizing Frost's compliment a little too carefully. Then we shall be reminded that human history is but a drop in the sea of geological history. And that is what scares—that is the true serial ordeal concealed beneath the false ordeal of being watched by the eyes from the crumbling ruins of old houses. The eyes are not really there; the *as if* is meant to underscore that fact. But the man who journeys with Frost (if he be a true knight) must see all around the poet's figures, must glimpse into the harshness beneath. He has to prove himself capable of first grasping and then maintaining the multiple visions built into the poet's context; must prove, as well, that he can shoulder the burden of the knowledge of human time, comprehended, as Frost insists, within the frame of geological time.

Then, as if to intensify the ordeal of such encompassing vision:

> As for the woods' excitement over you
> That sends light rustle rushes to their leaves,
> Charge that to upstart inexperience.
> Where were they all not twenty years ago?
> They think too much of having shaded out
> A few old pecker-fretted apple trees.

The animated woods might make us feel at home, for a brief moment, but the pleasure of such a welcoming is taken away as soon as it is given. The question "Where were they all not twenty years ago?" is enough to put them in their place, far below the abiding rock, implying that whatever has the spark of organic life, trees or humans, is, from the perspective of geological time, doomed to quick extinction. The rock remains, impervious to the gouging chisels of Glacier and wagon wheels, but the apple trees are vulnerable to the damage that woodpeckers can do—they are "pecker-fretted." The troubled apple trees stand alone as the last sentient objects in the insentient landscape projected in the poem, and as a hint of the landscape of human suffering that we soon discover in our trip up history's stream.

And now, approaching our destination, the poet directs us to engage our imagination:

> Make yourself up a cheering song of how
> Someone's road home from work this once was,
> Who may be just ahead of you on foot
> Or creaking with a buggy load of grain.
> The height of the adventure is the height
> Of country where two village cultures faded
> Into each other. Both of them are lost.
> And if you're lost enough to find yourself
> By now, pull in your ladder road behind you
> And put a sign up CLOSED to all but me.

In the face of all the barrenness, the imagination begins to infuse its life-giving powers into a long-dead human scene. The isolated and wandering knight of "Directive" needs something more than the promise of a special grail waiting for him, one of the right ones, at the end of his long journey. Bereft of community he begins to make his own in song (like whistling in the dark?); the precise and homely detail of "creaking with a buggy load of grain" is not a sentimental gesture but a projection from a mind made desperate by its needs of the comforts of common human realities. The height of adventure is not the finding of imagination's desired realities, but the finding of the vestiges of human culture. The height of adventure, to put it another way, is not the verification of imagination's humanizing illusions, but the pressing of imagination to its furthest reaches by the discovery of the final evidence of the abject sadness of the human condition in a human-repelling universe. Our climb up into the higher country is a metaphor for the journey of imagination (echoing the swinging metaphor from "Birches") and Frost is quick to seize upon the conceit buried in the idea of the old "ladder road" to emphasize that the final stage of a journey in the mind has been reached and that it is a journey that can be completed only by solitary men. The imagination pours forth its greatest

energies only after it has realized its anarchic potential, severing itself from
all connections: "CLOSED to all but me."

We have traveled far, passing through geological, cultural, and organic
time in our search for the serenity that the present could not give. Now
firmly situated in country hospitable only to the imagination, we must take
stock of what we have been given:

> Then make yourself at home. The only field
> Now left's no bigger than a harness gall.
> First there's the children's house of make-believe,
> Some shattered dishes underneath a pine,
> The playthings in the playhouse of the children.
> Weep for what little things could make them glad.
> Then for the house that is no more a house.
> But only a belilaced cellar hole,
> Now slowly closing like a dent in dough.
> This was no playhouse but a house in earnest.

It hardly seems credible that history's graveyard could be imagination's
proper place. All around are the signs of death and pain: the phrase "no
bigger than a harness gall," like the phrase "pecker-fretted apple trees,"
thrusts an image of suffering onto the natural landscape; better there than
someplace else. Actually, the galled and the fretted are those who threw up
against a hostile environment the "house in earnest," now a "belilaced cellar
hole" being sucked slowly into the earth—a fitting finale to the constant
mirror irritants, the little open sores which, like a harness gall, rarely claim
a life, just supply the daily portion of misery. The failed "house in earnest"—
an all too vulnerable enclosure—is opposed by the house that never was in
reality and therefore still is in "make believe"—an enclosure beyond assault.
What fascinates the poet most about this entire scene is not the image of
failure and futility, but those shattered, useless dishes that are the playthings
in the children's dreamy play world.

> Your destination and your destiny's
> A brook that was the water of the house,
> Cold as a spring as yet so near its source,
> Too lofty and original to rage.
> (We know the valley streams that when aroused
> Will leave their tatters hung on barb and thorn.)
> I have kept hidden in the instep arch
> Of an old cedar at the waterside

> A broken drinking goblet like the Grail
> Under a spell so the wrong ones can't find it,
> So can't get saved, as Saint Mark says they mustn't.
> (I stole the goblet from the children's playhouse.)
> Here are your waters and your watering place.
> Drink and be whole again beyond confusion.

The brook is our destination *and* destiny: both the end of the physical journey and the inevitable fated object of our imagination's teleological process. Unlike the valley stream which when swollen with spring rains can wreak destruction, the brook does not rage, does not disturb the life around it. It alone among natural forces harmonizes with human existence. Once the lifeblood of the house that is no more, now we are drawn to the waters of the brook as to the sacred waters of baptism. We have not, finally, traveled back through public history, but through private, inner time. What we recover, if we brave the various assaults that the poet has subjected us to, is the pristine moment of our childhood imagination—a moment that stands outside time—the embryo moment of our maturer imaginative faculty. Unfettered by ironic habits of vision, the mind of the child can build up out of the broken objects of the adult life the purer fantasies that occupy his days.

And now we return to that sacred source to renew ourselves, to make ourselves whole again, and to overcome the confusion we have left and to which we shall and must return. But if we would drink out of the goblet that is "like the Grail"—again the obtrusive simile drives home the ironic consciousness of the poet—then we must know that we drink from a broken goblet (hidden, appropriately, in the playhouse to which we must return to recover the root energies of adult imagination). Our transformation from confused adult to simple child is not complete and could not be complete. Yet this is what Frost's special kind of redemption has been all about, all along. The unself-conscious acts of child imagination foreshadow the deeply self-conscious imaginative visions of adult life. The child gives the example to the adult, for even as the children in play can transmute the shattered dishes into the fixtures of their magic world, so the adult, with examples of failure and suffering all around him, must somehow transform what he sees into a better world: we really have no choice—either we recreate the world better than it is, or we live an unbearable existence. We shall drink as much as a broken goblet will allow, even as we shall build up (but only within imagination's proper residence: the playhouse) a universe as humanized as the inhuman universe will permit. Perhaps the last lesson of a man of redemptive consciousness, of a self seeking to be "whole again beyond confusion," is that imagination's journey is ended only when the projection of imagination's shapes of hope and desire is accompanied by a sober self-consciousness that will keep us in touch with ourselves and the limits of our redemption, and keep us from projecting fantasy worlds that will spurn the law of gravity and spur us into anarchic solipsism.

RICHARD POIRIER

Choices

Frost could never blame the "age" for anything, or even blame what he did himself at a certain age for what might have happened to him subsequently. This was the virtue of his pride. Moral and literary accomplishment are of a piece in his poetry because of his near-mystical acceptance of responsibility for himself and for whatever happened to him. His biographer [Lawrance Thompson] misses this entirely. In his harsh, distorted, and personally resentful view of Frost's manipulative, calculating use of other people, Thompson sees only the determinations of a man who wanted fully to control his career and his public image. Unquestionably, that was one of the things he was doing. He was also revealing something wonderful about human life, or, if you wish, about his sense of what it was. He was communicating his conviction that, mysteriously, nothing happens to us in life except what we choose to have happen. A conscious "use" of other people, a conscious exploitation of them in order to be lazy, in order to get work done, or to get good reviews—this was at least making yourself, and others, aware of what you were doing. What is conspicuous about Frost's letters when he is asking for a favor is their uncommon forthrightness. There is in them the relish of self-exposure. He tries to make visible the choices he is making for his life, choices which were there anyway, invisibly at work on himself and on others. What he calls "the trial by existence" in the magnificent Dante-esque poem of that title in *A Boy's Will* is "the obscuration upon earth" of souls that have chosen to leave heaven and to accept

---

From *Robert Frost: The Work of Knowing.* © 1977 by Oxford University Press, Inc.

whatever human life might have in store for them. Even after a soul is saved, even after the "bravest that are slain" on earth find themselves in heaven, they discover another opportunity for bravery and choice, an opportunity all the more daring because the choice will not, once taken, even be remembered

> 'Tis of the essence of life here,
>   Though we choose greatly, still to lack
> The lasting memory at all clear,
>   That life has for us on the wrack
> Nothing but what we somehow chose;
>   Thus are we wholly stripped of pride
> In the pain that has but one close,
>   Bearing it crushed and mystified.

There are two kinds of choice here. We "greatly choose" some things and we "somehow chose" all the things that happen to us. The pride we may take in conscious choices is stripped away not by any obvious predominance of the unconscious ones but rather by our being ignorant of how much more inclusive they are. That is, the individual is denied the *privilege* of knowing that in fact no one else has made his life as it is. Frost was always seeking for the restitution of that lost and diminished sense of responsibility even while he was at the same time exalted by the mystery of not being able fully to grasp it. This divided consciousness helps explain the perplexing ways in which a poet who attaches so much value to form, with all the choice that involves, attaches equal value to freedom in the movement of the poem toward a form. The perplexity is not lessened by the fact that within the freedom there are the elements which he also "somehow chose." Thus he will write, in "The Figure a Poem Makes," that a poem "has an outcome that though unforseen was predestined from the first image of the original mood—and indeed from the very mood." For him, life and poems work in much the same way. In both, there is a wondrous emergence into consciousness of those selections, impressions—and choices—that were not available to consciousness when first made.

> The impressions most useful to my purpose seem always those I was unaware of and so made no note of at the time when taken, and the conclusion is come to that like giants we are always hurling experience ahead of us to pave the future with against the day when we may want to strike a line of purpose across it for somewhere. The line will have the more charm for not being

mechanically straight. We enjoy the straight crookedness of a
good walking stick. Modern instruments of precision are being
used to make things crooked as if by eye and hand in the old
days.

("The Figure a Poem Makes")

It is not stretching the point to say that this intimation of the peculiar
and mysterious workings of choice is what made him so resolute and even
ruthless when choice became incumbent or conscious. It was as if the free
movement in his life demanded of him that he then do what had to be done
either with his career, with a poem, or with a book. Despite differences, he
is in this more like Lawrence than like any other writer of the century. And
yet it seems apparent that form, for Lawrence as much as for Frost, the
more formalistic of the two, by being necessarily to some degree conscious
was also, to some degree, imposed, and that what Frost says about "modern
instruments of precision" might sometimes apply to his own work on a
poem. His claims, again in "The Figure a Poem Makes," to the "wildness
of logic" are apt to strike some readers as disingenuous. The "logic" of
even some of the best poems, as illustrated by "Spring Pools," does not, as
the reader experiences it, appear to be "more felt than seen ahead like
prophecy." Some of that, yes—but also a good deal of premeditation and
preplotting. Frost is best appreciated if we let him *try* to do the best he can
within the drama of form and freedom, and it is in that light that we can
understand the design he gave to *A Boy's Will* using some of the poems he
then had available. It is a matter of his using "experience," in this case
poems, that he had paved "the future with against the day when [he would
want] to strike a line of purpose across it for somewhere."

A *Boy's Will* is an appropriate place for a poem about choices of lives,
like "[The] Trial by Existence." The design of the book—what is put in,
what is left out, the groupings of the poems, the headnotes—expresses a
"choice" about the portrait of man and poet that Frost wanted to present.
Or rather what can be inferred from these "choices" of inclusion and exclusion are three portraits whose details sometimes coincide, sometimes blur,
sometimes block one another out. One, the cosiest, most availably public,
and closest to the glosses, is of a young man who develops a fulfilling
relationship to the world after passing through a period of alienation and
trial. Another is of a young man trying to shape the complex tension within
himself between sexuality and creative powers, between the calls of love
and of poetry. This is a more submerged portrait than the first, and its
features will remain both more indelible and more obscure all the way

through Frost's work. And then there is a darker version of this second portrait, a kind of *pentimento*, a possible portrait later painted over by an author who "repented" and wanted to block out certain features. He kept this portrait hidden, as it were, by the omission of a poem that could have fitted into this volume (bringing with it a darkening of all that would surround it) with at least as much effectiveness as it did into a later group that includes "Never Again Would Birds' Song Be the Same" and "The Most of It" in *A Witness Tree* of 1942. I am referring to "The Subverted Flower," the first draft of which had been written so early, if we are to believe what Frost himself told Thompson, that it could have been published in *A Boy's Will*.

Taken together these three overlapping portraits, while they do not account for all the poems in the volume—two of the best, "Mowing" and "The Tuft of Flowers," discussed [elsewhere]—do include most of them and the overall "plot" of the book. In discussing the alternate and interwoven portraits I want above all to insist that none of the features come inadvertently into prominence. Frost knew exactly what he was doing; he was never innocent of what his poems imply. His original omissions and discriminations are the result of his loyalty to the complex and mystifying way in which languages appropriate to sexuality, poetic practice, and nature are, in his consciousness of them, not to be separated one from the other. The elements of intentional disguise in any one of the tracings of the poetic self should not, that is, make anyone think that the other disguises, found beneath the obvious ones, were therefore unconscious. Frost was at once too doggedly responsible for whatever he did about himself and too mistrustful of himself and of his imagination ever to have said more than he knew.

Thompson's discussions of how the book was put together are at the outset too vague to be useful and too simple to be true. "Alone one night, he sorted through the sheaf of manuscripts he had brought with him and could not resist the impulse to see if he had enough to make up a small volume . . . [which] would represent his achievement up to the age of thirty-eight." "Impulse"? For one thing, he had far more than "enough" to make a book, and a better book than the one he put together. For another, what he did pick out for *A Boy's Will* did not begin to represent the variety, much less the size, of his accomplishment up to the age of thirty-eight. Evidence of this is in Thompson's own research into the dates of composition. No dramatic narratives are included in the book, for example, though at least three that were to appear the next year, 1914, in *North of Boston* had been written as early as 1905 and 1906—"The Death of the Hired

Man," "The Black Cottage," and "The Housekeeper." In addition, he had on hand over a dozen poems, all written before 1913, and including some of his best. "Bond and Free" was written in the period 1896–1900, and twelve more were written (or at least begun) in Derry between 1900 and 1911, including "An Old Man's Winter Night," "The Telephone," "Pea Brush," "An Encounter," "Range-Finding," "Loneliness," "The Line-Gang," "The Flower Boat," and "The Subverted Flower." In addition, some of the great sonnets were written during 1906–7: "The Oven Bird," "Putting in the Seed," and the fifteen-line sonnet variant "Hyla Brook." All these were held until the third book, *Mountain Interval*, in 1916.

Of course Frost may not have "brought with him" (the precise meaning, if any, of Thompson's phrase is never made clear) some of the poems destined for later printing. In that unlikely case, there would be a still stronger indication of some prior decision not to put into his first book works that would presumably fit better into some design of a poetic progress which was to be revealed in subsequent volumes. But there is no evidence that he did not have all of his manuscript poetry with him. Obviously he had to have the poems destined for *North of Boston* since this was printed before he left England. In fact, as soon as *A Boy's Will* was out, he began to play tricks with the whole revered critical notion of chronology and "development," using one of the poems he had had around since 1905–6. His specifically intended victim was also his most renowned admirer, Ezra Pound. Knowing that, when the facts became public, Pound, and the usual cant about newness, would be made to look silly, he gave him "The Death of the Hired Man" as a "new poem." After the publication in *Poetry* of his review of *A Boy's Will*, which Frost and his wife found condescending, Pound promised Harriet Monroe, the editor, that he would have something new from Frost "as soon as he has done it." "He has done a 'Death of the Farmhand' since the book [*A Boy's Will*]," he wrote his father on June 3, 1913, and adds with yet another example of his wholly engaging generosity of feeling, that this poem "is to my mind better than anything in it. I shall have that in *The Smart Set* or in *Poetry* before long". One thing is sure— that many of the poems held back were incomparably superior to at least three that he chose to publish but would eventually delete from later printings of his poems: "Spoils of the Dead," "In Equal Sacrifice," and "Asking for Roses." The last of these is a fair sample of all three. It is mildly interesting because it offers an early example of Frost's obsession with human dwellings that are impoverished and apparently deserted, and because it is a kind of *Lied* with echoes of Burns and Tom Moore. As the young lovers pass the house, they notice a garden of "old-fashioned roses":

> "I wonder," I say, "who the owner of those is."
> "Oh, no one you know," she answers me airy,
> "But one we must ask if we want any roses."

It is astonishing to learn, if Frost's own testimony is to be believed, that at the time he was willing to see in print this embarrassing poem about a man, a woman, and flowers, he held back "The Subverted Flower" which makes use of the same three items. The complex dramatic interaction between flowers (which are a symptom in the poems of seasonal fertility), sexuality, and poetry is one of the important but uninsistent lines of coherence in the volume. Frost's own awareness of it and of its implications is best indicated by his omission of a poem whose inclusion would have caused a substantial change of emphasis. It would have suggested very dark, psychological shadings in the sexual areas which, by the implications of Frost's language in his poetry and in his prose, provide some of the metaphors for artistic creativity. It would also have indicated that he was to some degree victimized by unrequited love and that his career was not as simple an unfolding of self as he wants to suggest.

From the outset "The Subverted Flower" establishes the powerful authority, the psychotic necessity, of its macabre imagery and the relentlessness of its movement. It is the sexual nightmare of an adolescent blankly registering the descent, through sexual repressions, of himself and the girl he desires into different forms of bestiality. The four-beat lines are rhymed in a staggered way that allows sudden accelerations past one fixation, like a nightmare image being recollected, on to the next, where we are suspended as in a trance until a disyllabic rhyme chooses to complete the frame. Except for a few of Meredith's sonnets in "Modern Love" there is little in any poetry before Frost that can approach the direct and graphic sexual terror of this poem, the first lines of which follow:

> She drew back; he was calm:
> "It is this that had the power."
> And he lashed his open palm
> With the tender-headed flower.
> He smiled for her to smile,
> But she was either blind
> Or willfully unkind.
> He eyed her for a while
> For a woman and a puzzle.
> He flicked and flung the flower,

And another sort of smile
Caught up like finger tips
The corners of his lips
And cracked his ragged muzzle.

The poem could refer to an incident of so-called indecent exposure in Frost's courtship of Elinor White, but the details make it likely that it is an account of a nightmare in which such an incident was symbolically enacted. This would be a good reason for his wanting to withhold it, and the probability that the poem has *something* to do with Elinor White is advanced by Thompson as the sole reason for Frost's delaying publication until 1942, after her death. The subject, Frost was later to say in his *Paris Review* interview, was "frigidity in women."

There are, however, complicated literary as well as personal reasons for his not having printed the poem in *A Boy's Will*, reasons that become apparent when we see that, except for its style, the poem would not have been out of place, and, oddly enough, would have easily fitted in thematically. The problem would have been that the poem excites a kind of autobiographical speculation that would have materially altered the "portrait of an artist" that Frost wanted to project. To begin with, the strangeness of the poem is considerably lessened once it is placed among those in *A Boy's Will* wherein flowers are a token of either a precarious movement toward sexual, seasonal, and artistic fulfillment or the failure of these. Or perhaps one should say that its strangeness informs and significantly alters these other poems. The volume as a whole begins with landscapes that are barren, even funeral, and in which the young man walks forth conspicuously alone. Following on the barren landscapes of the first three poems, "Into My Own," "Ghost House," and "My November Guest," whose name is Sorrow, we come upon the just-married couple of "Love and a Question." The bride and groom are visited by a tramp in need of shelter. The bridegroom turns him away from the door, and yet is peculiarly equivocal as he "looked at a weary road" while his bride sits behind him at the fire: "But whether or not a man was asked / To mar the love of two / By harboring woe in the bridal house, / The bridegroom wished he knew." Then in the next, or fifth poem, "A Late Walk," there is a faint signal of a new vitality. A "flower" is just barely rescued from the desolation which has dominated the scene up to that point. The young man is still, though married, walking alone amidst "withered weeds," bare trees, except for "a leaf that lingered brown." But his walk ends in a gesture of unification with what little is still alive in the landscape and with the life that awaits him at home: "I end not far from my going forth, / By picking the faded blue / Of the last remaining aster flower / To carry again to you."

From this point on, the isolated "I" who has only begun to express the intimacy of his feeling for "her" is replaced with "we" and "our." But the world continues nevertheless to be found cold and threatening. The next poem is "Stars" with its landscape of snow in which the lovers might be lost "to white rest and a place of rest / Invisible at dawn"—an accent of Emily Dickinson unusual for Frost. In the poem that follows, "Storm Fear," the young man still lies alone in his wakefulness, but he is apparently with his wife and fears not for himself so much as for her and the children. Following on these it is proposed in "Wind and Window Flower" that she is a "flower" and that he is a winter wind "concerned with ice and snow, / Dead weeds and unmated birds, / And little of love could know."

Even before this we have become aware that the threat to love has been gradually internalized by the young poet and that the landscape is an imaginary one of those moods, depressions, and melancholies which threaten their love with devastation and aridity. Only with the next four poems— "To the Thawing Wind" ("Give the buried flower a dream"), "A Prayer in Spring" ("Oh, give us pleasure in the flowers today"), "Flower Gathering," and "Rose Pogonias"—does the young poet escape from "dead weeds and unmated birds." Along with them the poet has himself been seen as a force for frigidity working in conjunction with the most malevolent aspects which he selects or imagines in the natural environment.

Though thematically "The Subverted Flower" could obviously belong to this grouping, it would have materially changed the implication of these poems insofar as they are about the nature of Frost's sexual-poetic imagination. By including it, Frost would have transferred responsibility from the young man to "her," or Elinor. As a result, he would have obscured the fact that the poems in this volume are essentially concerned with the connections between his poetic prowess and his power to find love within a landscape of the mind as well as in relation to another person. The poems trace out the effort to free his imagination so that it might work toward some harmony with natural cycles both of the seasons and of sexuality. With inclusion of "The Subverted Flower," the interest in the volume would have become more psychological than literary; it would have placed greater emphasis on the hazards of sexuality to the confusion of a Wordsworthian subject which more classically includes sexuality: the "Growth of a Poet's Mind." "The Subverted Flower" is not, as are the others, about *his* potentially frigid mind or imagination but about hers. His delicacy about Elinor White Frost was real enough, no doubt, but equally real was the desire to make himself responsible for anything that might have affected his poetry. It was Frost's enormous desire for control, form, design that forbade his including a poem which might imply, even by blaming another, that he was not the master of his literary fates.

The exclusion of this poem helps explain a number of things implied by his also having left out the other poems I have mentioned. First of all, the selection for A Boy's Will was not governed in any thoroughgoing way by the novelistic and self-revelatory scheme he himself claimed to have set up: "The psychologist in me," he was to say later on, "ached to call it 'The Record of A Phase of Post Adolescence' ". Second, the nature of the volume, and the determination of the order of poems, suggest other reasons for leaving out "The Subverted Flower," reasons having to do with Frost's imagination of a poetic career and with his fierce determination to control the public shaping of his life. He would rather have let at least some people think that part of the structure of A Boy's Will was dictated by "the seasons," which is superficially true, than allow most people freely to discover that the seasons are finally only a metaphor for the possible and always threatened perversion or subversion of the poetic imagination by the disasters of love. He would rather have pretended that the volume is about "A Phase of Post Adolescence" than have us ask if the connection in his work between sexuality and the progress of poetry is not far more complicated than he chooses to admit. Which is a way of saying that while he knew everything that was going on in his poetry he was not always anxious that we should know as much as he does.

Many of the early poems, offering some of the psychological and structural sources of all of Frost's poetry, are about this relation of love to poetic making, to making in all other senses of the word. A brief biographical digression might be useful here, a recapitulation of Frost's stormy and passionate courtship of Elinor White, with whom he seems to have fallen in love at first meeting. He was seventeen, she nearly two years older, and they sat next to one another in Lawrence High School (Massachusetts). From the outset, her ability as a poet (she stopped writing poems before she married him and in later life tried to disguise and disown those that had appeared in the School Bulletin), her knowledge of literature, her marks in school (they were co-valedictorians, but her average was finally higher), her ability as a painter, her suitors at St. Lawrence University at Canton, New York, all excited his competitive admiration and jealousy. Her attendance at college meant their separation, with Frost going to Dartmouth for a short

time, then to teach in the Methuen schools until March 1893, then to act
as helper and guardian to Elinor's mother and two of her sisters in Salem,
New Hampshire. Before she left for school and on her vacations in Lawrence
he courted her with the help of Shelley's poetry, especially "Epipsychidion,"
with its inducements to ignore the institution of marriage. And of course
he wooed her with poems of his own.

Indeed, his first volume, strictly speaking, was not *A Boy's Will* of
1913, when he was thirty-nine, but *Twilight* in 1894 when he was twenty,
the one surviving copy of which is in the Barrett Collection at the University
of Virginia. Only two copies were printed, one for Frost and one for Elinor.
It included, in addition to "My Butterfly" which was later to appear in *A
Boy's Will*, four other poems full of literary echoes ranging from Sidney to
Keats, Tennyson to Rossetti, as in the opening lines of the title poem:

> Why am I first in thy so sad regard,
> O twilight gazing from I know not where?
> I fear myself as one more than I guessed!

He carried Elinor's copy on an unannounced trip to her college boarding
house in Canton. Surprised, bewildered, prevented by the rules from inviting
him in or from going out herself, she accepted her copy in what seemed a
casual but was perhaps a merely preoccupied way. She told him to return
home at once. He did so, but only to pack a bag and leave for a suicide
journey that took him to Virginia and through the Dismal Swamp at night,
"into my own," so to speak. The danger was very real. "I was," he later
said, "trying to throw my life away." Through this and subsequent travails,
torments, threats, and melodramatic scenes, he convinced her to marry him
before she could finish school and before he had any secure means of
support.

Such briefly are the biographical elements probably at play in some of
the early poems. But the biographical material does not tell us as much
about the man as the poetry does. By that I mean that the poetry does not
necessarily come from the experiences of his life; rather, the kind of poetry
he wrote, and the kind of experiences to which he was susceptible, both
emerge from the same configuration in him, prior to his poems or to his
experiences. Sex and an obsession with sound, sexual love and poetic imagination, success in love and success in art—these conspire with one another.
A poem is an action, not merely a "made" but a "making" thing, and "the
figure a poem makes," one remembers, "is the same as for love." It is as if
in talking about the direction laid down by a poem he instinctively uses a
language of ongoing sexual action:

No one can really hold that the ecstasy should be static and stand still in one place. It begins in delight, it inclines to the impulse, it assumes direction with the first line laid down, it runs a course of lucky events, and ends in a clarification of life—not necessarily a great clarification such as sects and cults are founded on, but in a momentary stay against confusion.... It finds its own name as it goes and discovers the best waiting for it in some final phrase at once wise and sad—the happy-sad blend of the drinking song ("The Figure a Poem Makes").

Three early poems, "Waiting," "In a Vale," and "A Dream Pang," coming nearly in the middle of *A Boy's Will*, illustrate the connections, implicit in the structuring of the whole volume, between sexual love and poetic making, between the "sounds" of love and a poet's love of sound. None of the three is in any sense considerable. Frost's investment in them is relatively slight; they are shy of the complications which, when they emerge in later poems, are more consciously and subtly managed. And yet the poems are the stranger for *not* showing very much acknowledgment of their strangeness. It is as if initially the imagination of the sexual self and of the poetic self were so naturally, so instinctively identified as not to call for comment.

The three poems are published in sequence in *A Boy's Will*, always an important and calculated factor in Frost. They are all what can be called dream poems, and each suggests a different aspect of the dreamlike relationship between poetic and sexual prowess. In the first, "Waiting," the figure of the poet is "specter-like," as he wanders through a "stubble field" of tall haycocks, a bit like the "stubble-plains" in the last stanza of Keat's ode "To Autumn"; the "things" about which he has waking dreams are mostly the surroundings and their noises. From the outset his condition seems peculiarly vulnerable to sights and sounds, and it is not till the final lines that one can attribute this to the fact that what means most to him in his dream is not anything present to his senses but rather "the memory of one absent most," the girl he loves:

Waiting
Afield at Dusk

What things for dream there are when specter-like,
Moving among tall haycocks lightly piled,
I enter alone upon the stubble field,
From which the laborers' voices late have died,

And in the antiphony of afterglow
And rising full moon, sit me down
Upon the full moon's side of the first haycock
And lose myself amid so many alike.
I dream upon the opposing lights of the hour,
Preventing shadow until the moon prevail;
I dream upon the nighthawks peopling heaven,
Each circling each with vague unearthly cry,
Or plunging headlong with fierce twang afar;
And on the bat's mute antics, who would seem
Dimly to have made out my secret place,
Only to lose it when he pirouettes,
And seek it endlessly with purblind haste;
On the last swallow's sweep; and on the rasp
In the abyss of odor and rustle at my back,
That, silenced by my advent, finds once more,
After an interval, his instrument,
And tries once—twice—and thrice if I be there;
And on the worn book of old-golden song
I brought not here to read, it seems, but hold
And freshen in this air of withering sweetness;
But on the memory of one absent, most,
For whom these lines when they shall greet her eye.

Before the mention of his beloved, in the next to last line, the poem is filled with evocations of natural sounds in the "stubble field" where "the laborers' voices late have died"; there is also the "vague unearthly cry" of the nighthawks who plunge "headlong with fierce twang afar"; there are the "bat's mute antics," the "rasp" of a creature who "silenced by my advent, finds once more, / After an interval, his instrument." But what is apt to seem most provocative—given its place at the end of the poem and its uniqueness among all the references to natural sound—is an allusion to poetic sound, to the "worn book of old-golden song." It, too, is a carrier of sound, very likely of sound that helped (even more than did the sounds of nature) during his courtship of the one now "absent." But however much our literary-critical dispositions might prompt us to separate this item of sound from others, as being more centrally important, it is necessary to note that the young poet-specter tends merely to put the poetic within the sequence of other items. It is joined to them casually with another of the many "ands" that make up the listing. Apparently he does not intend even to read the book in order to bring her closer to mind. More than that, though the book is "worn" and though the poetry is itself "old," his reasons for holding onto it are that it may "freshen in this air," this Keatsian air "of withering sweetness."

The "old-golden song" is to be freshened, strangely enough, by something that is more apt to dry it, to "wither" it. We are readied by this paradox for the introduction, as in "Pan with Us," of the theme of "new" song, new sounds, something poetic for the future—in short, the very poem we are reading which is destined for her: "for whom these lines when they shall greet her eye." With the vitality of "shall greet her eye" the poet is no longer "specter-like." He has gotten past a number of by-ways: of possible dreams on other sounds, of the invitation to do no more than dream, of losing himself to these sounds—a danger only less intense than that in the later "Stopping by Woods on a Snowy Evening." Past all this, the young lover is able to envision a future in love inseparable from a future in poetry. He has been able to do this because, all the while, as the poem moves along, he has been "making it"; he has been writing "these lines."

One indication of the peculiar nature of Frost's reputation as a poet, when compared to an Eliot or a Yeats, is that few have bothered with poems so clearly not of his best like "Waiting" or the two others grouped with it. His admirers are defensively anxious to show only the favorite things, when some of the lesser ones are often even more revealing of his preoccupations with the plights and pleasures in the life of the poetic self. "In a Vale" is, even more than "Waiting," fin de siècle in conception and language. With its "vale," "maidens," "fen," and with words like "wist," "list," "dwelt," there is little going on that predicts the later Frost except the penultimate and best stanza. And yet it is still a most ingratiating poem—like an early picture of someone we have gotten to know only in later years—and it tells us perhaps even more than do more posed sittings:

> When I was young, we dwelt in a vale
>   By a misty fen that rang all night,
> And thus it was the maidens pale
> I knew so well, whose garments trail
>   Across the reeds to a window light.
>
> The fen had every kind of bloom,
>   And for every kind there was a face,
> And a voice that has sounded in my room
> Across the sill from the outer gloom.
>   Each came singly unto her place,

But all came every night with the mist;
　　And often they brought so much to say
Of things of moment to which, they wist,
One so lonely was fain to list,
　　That the stars were almost faded away

Before the last went, heavy with dew,
　　Back to the place from which she came—
Where the bird was before it flew,
Where the flower was before it grew,
　　Where bird and flower were one and the same.

And thus it is I know so well
　　Why the flower has odor, the bird has song.
You have only to ask me, and I can tell.
No, not vainly there did I dwell,
　　Nor vainly listen all the night long.

The time scheme of these poems is importantly suggestive of poetic gestations, of the way past and present provide the nutrients for a poetic future. In "Waiting" we are in the present, witnessing the impressions made upon a young poet who holds the past in his hand—Palgrave's *Golden Treasury*—while composing in his head the "lines" which will in future "greet" his beloved. "In a Vale" is a dream wholly of the past, but it, too, looks ahead to a future wherein the past will have been redeemed by the writing of the poems inspired by it: "You have only to ask me, and I can tell. / No, not vainly there did I dwell, / Nor vainly listen all the night long." The listening, again, is to voices or sounds that he has managed to supersede: "a misty fen that rang all night"; the voices that have "sounded in my room" and that "brought so much to say." The dream is a rather wet one ("the last went, heavy with dew") and it is from these nocturnal experiences that he learns what, in the later daytime of publication, he "can tell." With Lucretius, he can tell that "the bird and flower were one and the same." However, he can also tell a more American and Emersonian story: of a world, again, which reveals itself in forms (odor and song) which have in part been placed there by the human imagination, including human dreams.

An absent lover imagined in "Waiting" as a future reader, ghostly lovers or maidens whose sayings "In a Vale" will in some future time allow him to "tell" readers about birds and flowers—these figurations are brought together in the last of the three poems, "A Dream Pang." There the poet is discovered in bed with his lover beside him, her very presence proving that his song has been answered by something more fulfilling than the echoing sounds of nature. This early poem is thereby a prelude to later ones like "Come In" or "A Leaf-Treader," where Frost is in danger of succumbing to the call of nature, of losing himself, of having his sound in words absorbed into the sounds made by the natural elements. In this poem he is not learning to "tell" or expecting the "lines" he is writing to be read; here he is already a poet whose song, in his dream, has been endangered by her denials and by his proud withdrawals:

> I had withdrawn in forest, and my song
> Was swallowed up in leaves that blew alway;
> And to the forest edge you came one day
> (This was my dream) and looked and pondered long,
> But did not enter, though the wish was strong:
> You shook your pensive head as who should say,
> "I dare not—too far in his footsteps stray—
> He must seek me would he undo the wrong."
>
> Not far, but near, I stood and saw it all,
> Behind low boughs the trees let down outside;
> And the sweet pang it cost me not to call
> And tell you that I saw does still abide.
> But 'tis not true that thus I dwelt aloof,
> For the wood wakes, and you are here for proof.

Now, as she lies beside him ("this was my dream . . . you are here for proof") the poem can come to articulation; before, while they were alienated from one another, "my song / Was swallowed up in leaves." Without her, he and his song are lost to the vagaries of nature and its noises; with her, nature, or the "wood," comes to a more orderly life outside their place: "the wood wakes, and you are here." The implications take us to a variety of poems in which Frost can feel momentarily and terrifyingly included, as he says in "Desert Places," in the loneliness of nature "unawares." Cut off from the communion of human sex and human love, he is answered either by random, accidental, teasing responses, like that of the little bird in "The Wood-Pile," or by evidences of brutish indifference such as greet the speaker of "The Most of It":

> He would cry out on life, that what it wants
> Is not its own love back in copy speech,
> But counter-love, original response.
> And nothing ever came of what he cried

> Unless it was the embodiment that crashed
> In the cliff's talus on the other side.

The failure of love, of love-making, the failure to elicit "counter-love" means, as in "The Subverted Flower," that the young poet cannot finally be joined to that human communication with nature which Emerson promised might be found there. Here as elsewhere Frost's Emersonism is grounded in certain basic actualities, especially the sexual relations of men and women, which Emerson himself tended to pass over with little more than citation. Within this sequence of three poems, "A Dream Pang" looks ahead to the implications of a more considerable sequence of three poems, already mentioned, that includes "The Most of It," "Never Again Would Birds' Song Be the Same," and "The Subverted Flower." The implication, briefly noted also in "The Vantage Point," is that a man alone ("he thought he kept the universe alone") cannot see or hear anything in nature that confirms his existence as human. If he is alone, he cannot "make" the world; he cannot reveal himself to it or in it; he becomes lost to it; it remains alien. He cannot make human sound. In "The Subverted Flower" he can at first hope that the impasse " 'has come to us / And not to me alone.' " But even this proposition falls on deaf ears, or essentially deaf ears. It is something "she thought she heard him say; / Though with every word he spoke / His lips were sucked and blown / And the effort made him choke / Like a tiger at a bone."

In the early, as in the later sequence, Frost is concerned in various ways with the possibilities of the sounds of the man-poet-lover in situations where there are competing sounds and where, if he cannot "make it" with his beloved, he cannot "make it" either in competitions with sounds in nature or in other poetry. He cannot "make it" with words so shaped as to reveal his participation in poetry, and—equally important—that such participation is "natural." He is not content to have "*his* song" swallowed up in leaves either of a tree, merely, or of a book, merely. His poetry, his song, must include both.

In the light of this ambition we can best understand Frost's life-long commitment to certain theories of sound and poetic form. The commitment is implicit in all of the poems and in the structural organization of *A Boy's Will*. It was to find theoretical expression somewhat later, in letters written at the time of the publication of the book, and later still in essays and talks. In a letter to the black poet-critic-anthologist William Stanley Braithwaite, on March 22, 1915, for example, Frost said:

It would seem absurd to say it (and you mustn't quote me as saying it) but I suppose the fact is that my conscious interest in people was at first no more than an almost technical interest in their speech—in what I used to call their sentence sounds—the sound of sense. Whatever these sounds are or aren't (they are certainly not of the vowels and consonants of words nor even of the words themselves but something the words are chiefly a kind of notation for indicating and for fastening to the page) whatever they are, I say, I began to hang on them very young. I was under twenty when I deliberately put it to myself one night after good conversation that there are moments when we actually touch in talk what the best writing can only come near.... We must go into the vernacular for tones that haven't been brought to book. We must write with the ear on the speaking voice. We must imagine the speaking voice.

"Sentence sounds" does not refer to the meaning the words give to a sentence but to the meaning the sound of the sentence can give to the words, which is why Frost is so difficult to translate into any other language. It is a matter of stress patterns. Thus, the line "By June our brook's run out of song and speed" is arranged so that the potential of the word "song"—as a possible allusion to "poetry"—is markedly diminished by putting it immediately after the quickly paced vernacular phrase "run out of." The word "song" would be far more potent, but altogether too archly so, if it traded places with the word "speed": "By June our brook's run out of speed and song." Some of these distinctions are clarified in a letter written over a year before, February 22, 1914, to his friend John Bartlett, a newspaper man who was one of his favorite students at Pinkerton Academy:

I give you a new definition of a sentence:

A sentence is a sound in itself on which other sounds called words may be strung.

You may string words together without a sentence sound to string them on just as you may tie clothes together by sleeves and stretch them without a clothes line between two trees, but— it is bad for the clothes.... The sentence sounds are very definite entities. (This is no literary mysticism I am preaching.) They are as definite as words. It is not impossible that they could be collected in a book though I don't at present see on what system they would be catalogued.

> They are apprehended by the ear. They are gathered by the
> ear from the vernacular and brought into books. Many of them
> are familiar to us in books. I think no writer invents them. The
> most original writer only catches them fresh from talk, where
> they grow spontaneously.
>
> A man is all a writer if *all* his words are strung on definite
> recognizable sentence sounds. The voice of the imagination, the
> speaking voice must know certainly how to behave [,] how to
> posture in every sentence he offers.

When Frost refers to the "vocal imagination" (in the essay "The Constant Symbol") he makes it synonymous with what he calls "images of the
voice speaking." Frost listens for these images as much in nature as in human
dialogue. But there is an important difference in what he wants and expects
to hear from these two different places: only in human dialogue can such
images emerge as "sentence sounds" rather than as mere echoes, or vagrant,
only potentially significant noises, like "The sweep / Of easy wind and downy
flake," or what Thoreau calls "brute sounds." Furthermore, Frost's capacity
even to find "images of the voice speaking" in nature depends upon human
love; it can be crippled or thwarted by the lack of it. The matter might be
put in a three-part formula: (1) the "artist as a young man," if doomed to
"keep the universe alone," can only call forth from it alien and terrifying
sounds, and is in danger of becoming either a mere passive receiver of these
sounds or himself a brute; (2) the "artist as a young man" in a reciprocal
relationship of love with another human can, as a result, also find "images
of the voice speaking" in some rudimentary form in nature, though it is
important to know that what he finds is only an image, nothing wholly
equivalent to the human voice speaking: "The Need of Being Versed in
Country Things" is that one is thereby allowed "Not to believe the phoebes
wept." This brings up the third and most important point: (3) that the
clearest, but not only, differentiation of human sound from sounds in nature
is poetry itself, the making of a poem, the capacity literally to be "versed"
in the things of this world. Any falling—of leaves, of snow, of man, of the
garland of roses which Adam is holding when he first sees Eve in her fallen
state—can be redeemed by loving, and the sign of this redemption is, for
Frost, the sound of the voice working within the sounds of poetry. It could
even be said that the proper poetic image of the Fall and of the human will
continually to surmount it is—given accentual-syllabism's unique role in the
handling of English rhythm—the mounting from unstressed to stressed syllables in the iambic pentameter line. Thus, the oven bird can "frame" the

question of "what to make of a diminished thing" in "all but words." The words are at the call of the poet; the "making" is in his power. It consists precisely in his showing how the verse form works with and against mere "saying":

He sáys | thė eaŕlly̆ pétlȧl fáll | iṡ pást,
Whėn peár | and chérlry̆ bloóm | weṅt dówn | iṅ shówleṙs.

The glory of these lines is in the achieved strain between trochaic words like "early" and "petal," "cherry" and "showers," and the iambic pattern which breaks their fall. The meter is a perfect exemplification of what the poem is about, of the creative tension between a persistent rising and a natural falling—a poise of creativity in the face of threatened diminishments.

MARIE BORROFF

Robert Frost's New Testament:
The Uses of Simplicity

Nothing about the language of Robert Frost has been more often remarked on than its simplicity, a quality doubtless more striking in the earlier
than the later poems, yet nonetheless integral to our ideas of Frost and his
style. I propose to consider this quality, as manifested specifically in diction
or choices among words, in some well-known poems taken mainly from
Frost's first three volumes, *A Boy's Will* (1913), *North of Boston* (1914),
and *Mountain Interval* (1916); I shall explore some of its observable, factual
implications and go on to show how these bear on broader questions of
dramatic strategy and structure. The insights thus gained can usefully be
applied to later poems of Frost's in which the language is not so simple, as
I hope to demonstrate in a concluding analysis of an important and notably
difficult late poem, "Directive."

The most obvious, objective correlative of "simplicity" in language is
word length—the frequency, for instance, of lines made up wholly of monosyllables, and a corresponding infrequency of words of three syllables or
more. This can conveniently be illustrated from two passages on the theme
of moral transiency, the former from "The Lesson for Today," one of Frost's
Horatian, discursive pieces, the latter from the perceptibly "simpler" lyric
"The Strong Are Saying Nothing":

> There is a limit to our time extension.
> We all are doomed to broken-off careers,
> And so's the nation, so's the total race.

From *Language and the Poet: Verbal Artistry in Frost, Stevens, and Moore.* © 1979
by The University of Chicago. The University of Chicago Press, 1979.

The earth itself is liable to the fate
Of meaninglessly being broken off.
(And hence so many literary tears
At which my inclination is to scoff.)
Wind goes from farm to farm in wave on wave,
But carries no cry of what is hoped to be.
There may be little or much beyond the grave,
But the strong are saying nothing until they see.

A more interesting factual reflection of "simplicity" or "difficulty" in language may be found in word origins. Compared with the second passage just quoted, the first four lines of the first poem contain twice as many words belonging to two etymological categories, roughly equivalent to "derived from French" and "derived from Latin," which I shall call "Romance" and "Latinate"; more significantly, the first four lines of the first poem contain five Latinate words, the second none. Samplings of texts from the sixteenth century to the present, representing the widest possible range of subjects and genres, indicate that successive Romance-Latinate percentiles of below 10, counting every word seriatim in 100-word sequences, represent the "low" extreme for English style. I have never found a 100-word sequence containing no Romance or Latinate elements at all, except, of course, where an author has deliberately excluded them as Joyce did at the beginning of his philological tour-de-force in the "Oxen of the Sun" episode of *Ulysses*, or as Edna St. Vincent Millay did in *The King's Henchman*. Percentiles of under 5 are rare even in markedly "low" styles, and percentiles below 10 regularly correlate with an impression of plainness and simplicity such as we associate with Frost (though in some styles, for example, that of E. E. Cummings, odd collocations of words or eccentric syntax may produce an "overlay" of opacity).

The statistically low extreme in Frost as regards Romance and Latinate diction seems to be represented by "Mending Wall," and I should like to begin my investigation of the relation between language and dramatic structure with this poem. Here a disclaimer is perhaps in order. It is not my view that tabulations of linguistic detail will of themselves yield an understanding of the all-important relationship between what a poem expresses and how it is expressed. But given the critic's initial grasp of what is going on in a poem—its "meaning" in the fullest sense of that term—he can both enlarge his understanding and enhance his sense of the poem as an object by paying some attention to the verbal materials of which it is made, coming to see more clearly "within the illumined large, / The veritable small," and discovering how a certain kind of verbal material can itself be an important determinant of poetic form.

The plot of "Mending Wall" is of course concerned with the opposed attitudes of the speaker and his unnamed "neighbor ... beyond the hill" toward the annual task of mending the stone wall between their adjoining farms, which is damaged every spring when the thawing earth heaves beneath it. The speaker views with humorous detachment the set procedure whereby each moves along his side of the wall putting back whatever stones have fallen into his field; the neighbor, however, takes it wholly seriously. The speaker is thus in sympathy with the force working from within the ground which "doesn't love a wall"; this attitude is also the poet's, and the reader is invited to share in it. But there is a second agency damaging to walls which the speaker is careful to distinguish as quite "another thing": the efforts of the hunters to "please the yelping dogs" by pulling apart the stones behind which a rabbit has taken refuge. This anti-wall agency is characterized by the bearing of weapons and the intention of destroying life (an explicit statement of the disapproval which remains implicit here appears in "The Rabbit Hunter"). It is thus to be associated with the image of the pro-wall neighbor as he looms in sight toward the end of the poem, "bringing a stone grasped firmly by the top / In each hand, like an old-stone savage armed." The natural gaps made in the wall each spring are large enough so that "two can pass abreast" through them; the image suggests friends or lovers sharing an excursion, as in "Two Look at Two." This sort of companionship is quite "another thing" from that of the speaker and his neighbor, who keep the wall between them as they go. An opening reference to the "spilling" of boulders "in the sun" carries implications of warmth and wastefulness, a sort of spring delight in disorder. The season also brings rising spirits, a groundswell of inner exuberance. "Spring is the mischief in me," the speaker says, and his association with the natural source of the gaps in the wall is thereby reinforced, for later in the poem he considers telling his neighbor they are the work of elves. He himself at one point essays a bit of puckish humor ("My apple trees will never get across / And eat the cones under his pines, I tell him"), but this brings forth no response. The solemn progress down the wall of the two neighbors is, to be sure, likened to a "game," but even here there is a hint of conflict: *side* in "one on a side" means, in the context of the figure, not only "direction in space" but "opposing faction." The line "to each the boulders that have fallen to each" expresses a sort of talion, an Old Testament-like law of equal remuneration, while the use of "spells" to make the replaced stones stay where they are evokes a superstitious past. So, too, the "darkness ... / Not of woods only and the shade of trees" in which the neighbor's figure is finally seen implies, in context, a benighted primitive era prior to the establishment of amicable social bonds.

By the end of the poem, there has emerged a constellation of related elements: warmth, exuberance, playfulness, humor—and, in opposition to the violence and hostility implicit in the acts of the hunters and in the image of the neighbor as an armed savage, the further and central values of sympathy, harmony, and reconciliation. The literal wall comes to stand for all antagonistic or mistrustful barriers dividing man from man (as well as from other creatures); that which does not love such a wall is, most important, the recurrent human impulse to reach out in sympathy toward other human beings, an impulse identified with the force which thaws the ground in spring. (One thinks of other poems by Frost, such as "A Prayer in Spring" and "Putting in the Seed," where the equation of love on human and natural levels is explicit.) The wall-destroying process is seen as a working from within the earth, gathering upward and spilling out; a widening movement antithetical in character to the verbatim repetition of a cautionary saying from one generation to the next. The poem ends in further repetition, unable to go beyond the saying just as its speaker is unable to get his idea across, either literally or figuratively, to his neighbor. The form of the ending enacts the walling in (or out) which is the negatively viewed component of the theme. But we must distinguish between what the speaker is trying to convey and what he wants to do. It is obvious from his reference to having "made repair" after the visitations of the rabbit hunters that he has no intention of literally allowing the wall to fall apart. The story told in the poem is not about a one-man rebellion against wall mending but about an attempt to communicate. The impulse to communicate and the content of the message itself are integrally related; as his means of communication, the speaker eschews direct statement in favor of appeals to the imagination and sense of humor. The action dramatized in the poem inevitably merges into the act of the poet in writing it.

I said earlier that "Mending Wall" seems to represent a low extreme for Frost in Romance-Latinate content. The poem is 398 words long; of these, 14 are Romance (*pass, rabbit, please, mending, line, use, balance, stay, turned, mischief, firmly, savage, armed, moves*) and 8 are Latinate (*repair, just, cones, fences, notion, offense, exactly, fences*). The percentiles for the four successive 100-word sequences (counting the last 98 words as 100) are 5, 6, 5, and 6. The question arising from this set of facts may be put in terms of either causes or effects. On the one hand, what motives or tendencies operate to keep the Romance-Latinate level so low? On the other hand, what dramatic significance or effectiveness does this sort of language have in the poem?

In answering the first question, it is necessary to admit at once the importance of "subject matter," understanding by this, however, not the plot or conception of the poetic drama, but the successive descriptive details through which this plot is developed. Of the concrete terms denoting persons and things belonging to the scene, not only *wall* but *ground, boulders, hunters, stone, dogs, neighbor, hill, pine, apple, orchard, trees, cows,* and *woods* are native; only *rabbits, fences,* and *cones* are Romance or Latinate. The names of country things in English are, for good cultural-historical reasons, for the most part of native derivation; it seems doubtful whether a poet representing in concrete detail an urban world of business offices, cocktail parties, and traffic jams could write poems with Romance-Latinate counts as low as this of Frost's. So far, then, subject matter might be said to "compel" the use of a certain kind of language. But we should observe that the words in "Mending Wall" denoting things referred to in similes and metaphors—things not properly part of the subject matter of the poem— also show a discernible bias toward native origins. The speaker describes the mysterious anti-wall force as a *groundswell* rather than a *surge;* he calls the differently shaped stones *loaves* and *balls* rather than *ovals* and *spheres;* wondering what to say to his neighbor, he thinks of *elves* but not of *fairies, goblins,* or *spirits.* The only such word not of native origin is *savage,* and as if to balance this, there occurs immediately preceding it a striking "translation" of Latinate *paleolithic* into native *old-stone.*

The argument from subject matter is always treacherous, for any subject can be treated in English, etymologically speaking, in more than one kind of language. It is amusing and instructive to think of equivalents for lines and passages of Frost's simple style, substituting as many Romance and Latinate words as possible while keeping the whole coherent. A student of mine once suggested, as an alternative for the opening of "Mending Wall," "There exists an antipathy toward barriers." One could continue by saying that this antipathy "causes an upward surge in the ground which creates apertures sufficiently large so that two people can pass through them simultaneously," and so on. The opening of "The Oven Bird" might similarly be rendered as: "There exists a species of bird, familiar to all, whose piercing note, sounding deep in the forest at the mid-point of the summer season, reverberates from the solid tree trunks." The well-known conclusion of "Hyla Brook," "We love the things we love for what they are," could be turned into "Our love of the object of love is based upon its nature in reality." The effect of all such translations is, needless to say, bathetic, if only because the music of the original lines is lost. But aside from this, the substitute versions throw into relief a perceptible stylistic quality of the originals which may be put under the heading of "manner" as opposed to "matter." As has often been noted, the speaker of Frost's poems gives the impression of talking or thinking spontaneously, rather than of uttering a prefabricated discourse which by its very form lays implicit claim to cultural importance. The revamped versions of "Mending Wall" and "The Oven Bird" sound, by contrast, like excerpts from texts on geology and ornithology, and the conclusion of "Hyla Brook" might be a key tenet in a treatise on ethics.

In addition to expressing a certain descriptive subject matter and implying a certain manner, Frost's plain and simple language is functional in a third, less obvious way. This can be demonstrated by comparing "Mending Wall" itself with such an explicit statement of the poem's theme as I presented earlier in this study. Among the more important words used to express the conceptual content latent in action and descriptive detail, *life, love, mistrustful, playfulness,* and *warmth* are native, but *antagonistic barriers, destruction, disorder, exuberance, force, harmony, hostility, human, humor, impulse, lavishness, natur(al), reconciliation, sympathy, violence,* and *wastefulness* are Romance or Latinate. Of these, all except *barriers, force, lavishness,* and *wastefulness* are Latinate. Of the words listed, only *love* occurs in the poem. As in "After Apple-Picking," the abstract terms that inevitably appear in an interpretation of the poem are absent from the poem itself. They are implied by factual statements ("We keep the wall between us as we go") or offhand comparisons ("Oh, just another kind of outdoor game, / One on a side"). When the speaker finds it necessary to point verbally toward the invisible forces and moral qualities which are in a sense the real subject of the poem, he takes refuge in the indefinite pronoun, as explained earlier, or in negative statement ("He moves in darkness . . . *not* of woods *only*"). "I could say 'Elves' to him," he thinks, "but it's *not* elves *exactly,* and I'd rather / He said it for himself." The poet clearly prefers that his reader should do the same.

We have observed that a translation of the simple language of "Mending Wall" and other poems of Frost's into heavily Romance-Latinate English produces an effect of prefabricated discourse, whereas the language of the originals sounds like spontaneous talk or thought. The reason for this is to be found in the history of the English language—or, more exactly, in the historical processes responsible for the transmission of the English language, as of any other, from one period to the next. In order that words may descend, they must be learned anew by successive generations of speakers, and different words are learned on different sorts of occasions—on different levels of use. Any educated man has in his vocabulary certain words which he may never have spoken, or heard spoken, on everyday occasions—words which he has learned from books or other formal modes of discourse, and which he uses, if he uses them at all, as an author or lecturer. These are "distinctively formal" words, transmitted in the language exclusively or mainly at the literary level of use. At the other extreme, there are words which we learn by hearing them used in everyday speech, and which we are not likely to meet in books except as the language of fictional forms mirrors the language of everyday. These are "distinctively colloquial" words, transmitted exclusively or mainly at the colloquial level or in an author's simulation of it. Between these two extremes lies the "common" level to which most words belong. Such words are "common" to literary and colloquial use alike, as well as "common" in the less technical sense of being frequently used and hence well known. They are generally lacking in distinctive stylistic qualities; this is because such qualities depend upon restrictions in range of use over a period of time. They are chameleon-like, standing out neither as conspicuously folksy or talky in literary contexts nor as conspicuously pretentious in colloquial contexts.

Now the formal word belongs to the public domain of cultural importance, including not only literature in all its forms, but government, law, religion, and other social institutions. The body of Romance loan words in English is, in the main, associated with the dominance of the Norman French and their Anglo-French descendants, during the Middle English period, in government and in the cultural establishment generally. The Latinate loanword group consists of words borrowed from literary, chiefly classical Latin during and after the Middle English period, by French and English writers who had learned them from books long after classical Latin had parted company with the popular spoken Latin which was to evolve into the Romance vernaculars. It is these aspects of cultural history which are responsible for the correlation between elevated stylistic quality in English words and Romance and, especially, Latinate origin. And it is this correlation, in turn, which gives the etymological analysis of passages of English text its potential value for the study of style. A further correlation, that between Latinate origin and abstractness of meaning, is illustrated by the above list of words significant in a thematic explication of "Mending Wall." In this respect, too, the expressive powers of words are determined in the course of time by the contexts in which they are used and the levels at which they are transmitted. The definition and discussion of abstract concepts are associated primarily with "the public realm of cultural importance," notably in such of its branches as science, religion, and philosophy. In contrast, the distinctively colloquial level of language grows out of, and reflects back upon, the world of everyday existence, a practically oriented world of physical activities directed toward concrete objects.

To sum up: through etymological breakdowns, we may corroborate our impression that a number of Frost's best-known early lyrics are made of a language from which distinctively formal words are largely excluded. But it is equally true and important—although for this, etymological breakdowns cannot provide objective corroboration—that the language of these poems is lacking in words and expressions of distinctively colloquial quality. If Frost does not say "There exists an antipathy toward barriers," neither does he say "Seems like there's something that's down on walls." He says that the annual mending of the wall "comes to" little more than a game, not that it "doesn't amount to" much more. (We should note that in this instance the general correlation between word origin and stylistic quality does not hold, the Romance word *amount* as used here being more, rather than less, colloquial than native *come*.) The poem does contain a few of the contracted phrases which are more characteristic of the colloquial than of the formal level of language ("doesn't," "isn't," "I'd," "it's"), but the number of corresponding full forms it contains is larger ("I have," "they have," "no one has," "do not," "he is," "spring is," "will not"). What is true of "Mending Wall" we find true elsewhere in Frost. The regionalisms so paradoxically lacking in poems so thoroughly regional are but one subclass of the distinctively colloquial elements of the English vocabulary which, with the distinctively literary elements, are by and large excluded. Frost's elected norm of discourse here, and the key to his verbal artistry, is the common level of style, which represents a selection from the spoken language rather than a reproduction of it. (One is reminded of Wordsworth's claim, in the preface to the 1800 edition of *Lyrical Ballads*, that he used "*a selection of* the real language of men" [emphasis added].) At the common level, the associations of words with both literary and colloquial realms are strongly maintained in the life of the language. Such words are forever ascending and descending the Jacob's ladder that connects the concrete and abstract dimensions of meaning. They are "common," too, in the more general sense; they seem simple because we know them so well, and they carry with them into abstract meanings something of the solidity of the world of everyday. Readily understood in context as a short form of *stone wall*, the word *wall* has the power of signifying a particular thing, familiar in structure and appearance. Through its equally familiar figurative uses in such expressions as "tariff wall" or "wall of indifference," it can lend itself to the process whereby the literally signified object takes on moral and emotional significance. The end product is not verbal but conceptual; not metaphor but symbol.

Stylistic effects, it must always be remembered, depend on the cooperation of many features as contributory causes. The characteristic diction of "Mending Wall" and other similar poems is one important aspect of a seemingly realistic style in which features of syntax, word order, and sentence structure drawn mainly from the common level also play their parts. In this style, too, the meanings of words and the content of successive statements are readily intelligible, even though the thematic interrelationships and implications of the statements may be subject to dispute. Nothing on the verbal surface is eccentric, illogical, or cryptic; there are no difficult metaphors or sophisticated plays on words: the references to stones as *loaves* and *balls* and the metonymy "He is all pine and I am apple orchard" are immediately understood because they are the sort of figures of speech we ourselves might use in conversation. All these aspects of style combine in an artful simulation of straightforward thought or speech which has at the same time a preternatural lucidity. Quite dissimilar effects have been produced by other poets using the same diction—by Housman in "Loveliest of trees, the cherry now / Is hung with bloom along the bough," by Cummings in "anyone lived in a pretty how town / (with up so floating many bells down)," by Thomas in "Time held me green and dying / Though I sang in my chains like the sea."

If diction is only one element of style, it is equally true that style is only one element of the poem. The artistry which made "Mending Wall" famous includes, it goes without saying, the power to compose sequences of lines which seem to speak themselves, lines in which dramatically expressive patterns of phrasing, intonation, and stress coexist miraculously with metrical form. Frost set great store by what he called his "sentence sounds," and indeed seems to have considered the ability to create them the one indispensable poetic gift. Yet the verbal power of a poet of Frost's stature is less than the architectonic power through which details of scene and action are made to assume dramatic force, so that the literal story, told with the utmost simplicity, gathers meaning as it unfolds without ever seeming staged. At such moments as that when the stone-bearing neighbor, approaching in darkness on the far side of the wall, metamorphoses in the speaker's thought into a caveman, the shaping hand of the artist disappears from view entirely, and we are struck as if by the portentousness of an event in real life.

I have so far discussed "Mending Wall" and other poems as if the style in which they are written never departed from the common level. In fact, Frost skillfully exploits the potentialities of the common style as a staging area for excursions upward or downward: pitched between literary and colloquial levels, it can be modulated either way without an obtrusive break. In Frost's hands, it dips occasionally to the distinctively colloquial level of everyday talk, as in the remark "Spring is *the mischief* in me" in "Mending Wall" or the pregnant question "what to *make of* a diminished thing" in "The Oven Bird." It is embellished with an occasional poetic or biblical archaism of native derivation (*o'er night* and *henceforth* in "The Tuft of Flowers," *ere* in "Putting in the Seed"), or archaic construction ("knew not" in "Mowing") or inversion of word order ("Something there is" in "Mending Wall"). But more significant than these for the thematic structure of Frost's poems is the exploitation of a body of words of native origin belonging to the common level of English diction, which have traditionally Christian associations, particularly with the Authorized Version of the Bible. An early sign that we may expect allusiveness of this sort in "Mending Wall" is the echo in line 7 of Matthew 24:2 (cf. Mark 13:2, Luke 21:6), "There shall not be left here one stone upon another." I have suggested that the line "to each the boulders that have fallen to each" expresses a sort of talion or Old Testament law of exact retaliation, and, in fact, the values of sympathy and reconcilement symbolically asserted in the poem are related to the prudential values of wall-maintaining much as, in Christian thought, the New Testament ethic of love is held to be related to the Old Testament ethic of justice, not so much superseding as broadening and deepening it. In such a setting the Christian connotations of certain salient words, given the reader's conscious or unconscious memory of them, are set vibrating. The *darkness* in which the neighbor is said to appear carries a suggestion of the spiritual state signified by that word in such texts as Matthew 4:16: "The people which sat in darkness" (cf. Luke 1:79); and John 1:5: "And the light shineth in darkness; and the darkness comprehended it not." Of major importance are the associations with the Christian ethic of the word *neighbor*, notably in the parable of the Good Samaritan with its final question, "Which . . . was neighbor unto him that fell among the thieves?" (Luke 10:36); and, of course, in the second of the two great commandments given by Christ in Matthew 22:37–39 (see also Mark 12:29–31; Luke 10:27): "Thou shalt love thy neighbor as thyself." The allusiveness of its final word gives to the concluding "saying" an additional dimension of ironic force.

The Christian religion is of course a part of "the public domain of cultural importance" which is also the domain of the distinctively formal in language. In its Christian allusiveness, Frost's language thus takes on a formality marked not by Romance and Latinate words but by words of native origin. And in so doing, it associates itself with what may be called the "high formal" tradition, marked out within the formal tradition generally by solemnity of tone. "High formality," in language as in other aspects of social behavior, serves to perpetuate time-honored cultural values by imputing dignity to the subject matter it treats; in some writers, it serves to confer authority on a new vision. High formality in language cuts across genres; it is found consistently in the language of religion; it is present uniformly or sporadically in the language of the law, of government, and of public oratory; it is what we know as the "high style" in the classical canon of English poetry. Much high formal language in English contains high percentiles of Romance and Latinate diction. ... But there is a branch of high formal language in English that is characterized by extremely low Romance-Latinate percentiles, and such language also tends to have the biblical allusiveness I have pointed out in certain passages of "Mending Wall." The tradition exemplified by these passages is Christian in origin and significance; its arch-exemplar for us is the Authorized Version of the Bible, and we find it also in Herbert's *The Temple*, Bunyan's *Pilgrim's Progress*, and Blake's *Songs of Innocence*. It complements and contrasts with the high formal tradition characterized by elaborate diction and syntax. Each of the two traditions is exemplified in certain texts in comparatively "pure" form: Donne's sermons and devotional prose are consistently elaborate in style, while *Pilgrim's Progress*, as noted, is consistently simple. But they may also be combined, as they are in *Paradise Lost*, where Milton modulates with unfailing mastery between the extremes of simplicity and elaboration.

I have traced out some of the implications of "simplicity" in Frost in terms of a statistically verifiable generalization, namely, that the language of certain poems has an extremely low Romance-Latinate content. One cause of this is the descriptive subject matter of the poems, a series of details referring to country things which tend to be designated by words of native origin. If we now turn from Romance-Latinate diction statistically considered to an examination of the particular Romance and Latinate words used—a complementary procedure essential for a full interpretation of the statistical results themselves—we find something more. In certain poems, such words play a distinct part in the thematic dramatization of the poet's world, having a "saliency" which outweighs their importance as "items." A particularly striking case is "Mowing."

If we read this poem with attention to the stylistic qualities of its language, we note a fluctuation in lines 9–12:

> Anything more than the truth would have seemed too
>   weak
> To the earnest love that laid the swale in rows,
> Not without feeble-pointed spikes of flowers
> (Pale orchises), and scared a bright green snake.

The diction of these lines departs in two directions from Frost's norm of the common and familiar. *Swale*, here a shortened form of *swale hay* or *swale grass*, would seem to be a local farmers' term; it implies the marshy ground on which both pale orchises and snakes are likely to thrive. *Orchises* is a learned word, whose collocation with *pale* results in an image that is, for Frost, unwontedly "poetic." We note also that the native word *weak* in line 9 is succeeded by its slightly more literary synonym *feeble*, of Romance origin, in line 11. Statistics alone, though they overstate the case, might have drawn our attention to the passage; six words out of nine in the little description of the orchises are Romance or Latinate, almost as many as occur in the first 100 words of the poem. The elevated quality of the language here is thrown into relief by the language preceding and following it. *Scare*, in the reference to the snake, is more colloquial than *frighten* (which is also of native origin) and has the additional value of a specific association with wild animals in the sense "cause to take flight (by startling)."

What is especially interesting about the cluster of Romance-Latinate elements in lines 11–12 is its relation to what is happening in the poem. Its appearance corresponds to the perception of something irrelevant to the task in which the speaker is engaged, something of aesthetic rather than economic value. Yet the inclusion of this perception in the meaning of the task is insisted on. The "earnest love" that wields the scythe repudiates mere wishful thinking, fairy-tale dreams of idleness and "easy gold," but it includes the orchises and the bright green snake. They, too, are implicitly part of the facts that labor knows and, hence, part also of the love and the sweetness of labor's self-fulfilling dream. In portraying a widening out of strictly practical into imaginative values, "Mowing" turns out to be reminiscent of "Mending Wall," and it suggests the other poem too in the speaker's wish to leave the message tacit, "whispered" but not spoken. Here again, what the speaker is shown as thinking or saying merges into the poet's act in writing the poem. The verb *to make* has long-standing associations in English with the writing of poetry, translating as it does the Greek verb which is the basis of the word *poetry* itself. At the end of the poem, the hay is left "to make" in the technical sense of becoming fit for stacking as a result of the drying action of the sun (see *OED* s.v. "make," v.[1], sense 38). The drying grass is a "fact" in the Latin sense of "something done"; both it and the poem itself remain as tangible, non-discursive legacies of the farmer-poet's love of his double task.

Close examination of language here leads to an insight into dramatic form which, tested out on other poems, proves valid for them as well. The central figure of these poems is shown at work on the farm he himself owns and maintains. His dutiful performance of an economically necessary task in a "workaday world" is the *donnée* of the poetic drama, but the performance of the task yields an unanticipated return in the form of an "earned" enhancement of experience—the perception of something having a beauty or meaning irrelevant in practical terms. The two—labor and its imaginative reward—are interdependent. Without the moment of perception, the task would be stultifying, but it is the carrying out of the task which makes the moment of perception possible. The swale must be mowed in order for the pale orchises and bright green snake to appear.

In "The Tuft of Flowers," a second character is incorporated into a similar plot: the change in the speaker's thought follows from his sympathetic understanding of the experience of the laborer who has preceded him in the field. The role of aesthetically or disinterestedly perceived object is taken over by the butterfly and, in turn, by the spared tuft of flowers, a "leaping tongue of bloom" which, like a Pentecostal tongue of flame, communicates the message made explicit in the poem's conclusion. So, too, in "Putting in the Seed," the "white / Soft petals fallen from the apple tree" are part of the speaker's experience, along with the peas and beans he is planting. (It is significant for our purposes that *seed*, *pea*, and *bean* are native words, while *petals* is Latinate.) The petals are irrelevant in practical terms; they are not seeds, although he is "burying" them (thus actually experiencing the "softness" of which he speaks). Yet neither are they "barren"; on the contrary, they are an inseparable part of that "springtime passion for the earth" which "burns through" the prosaic motions of the task.

The tragic story told in "Out, Out—," a poem Frost never would read aloud because it was "too cruel," is predicated on the denial of this process whereby labor becomes one with love. The narrow viewpoint of the adults, the "they" for whom the boy is working, is implied from the beginning in the speaker's description of the scene:

> And from there those that lifted eyes could count
> Five mountain ranges one behind the other
> Under the sunset far into Vermont.

Here the phrase "lifted eyes" ("raised their eyes" would have been equally satisfactory metrically, and perhaps more idiomatic) is reminiscent of Psalm 121:1, "I will lift up mine eyes unto the hills." The point is that "they" do not lift their eyes; the sunset is ignored. The boy is not allowed that extra "half-hour" at the end of the day that would have meant so much, and it is during this enforced continuation of work that the accident occurs which maims him and then ends his life. "They" are thus responsible; it is significant that the boy appeals not to "them," but to his sister, to save his hand when the doctor comes. The loss of the hand is obviously ironic in that it renders the boy useless for work: "No more to build on there." He now sees "all spoiled," but all is spoiled at the outset in a world dominated by so rigid a work ethic; life in such a world is indeed, in the Shakespearean phrase alluded to by the title, "a tale . . . signifying nothing." At the end of the poem, the speaker, far from indicating approval of "their" stoical acceptance of bereavement, dismisses them with contempt as they turn to their "affairs."

We have found basic to the dramatic structure of several of Frost's best-known early poems a process whereby the "economic and imaginative dimensions of experience," as we may somewhat pretentiously term them, are made one, the latter growing out of and depending on the former. The sequence of events in "Out, Out—" can be viewed as a thwarting of this process fraught with tragic consequences for an innocent party. Here, the separation between economic and imaginative dimensions is willfully imposed; in other poems it is more deeply founded—necessitated, it would seem, by the conditions of human life itself. In what is probably Frost's most famous poem, "Stopping by Woods on a Snowy Evening," the pressure of distant responsibilities, referred to in abstract terms, prevents the speaker from lingering to contemplate a sensuously appealing landscape near at hand. In his longing for the darkness and sleep represented by the "lovely" woods, swept by "easy wind and downy flake," he seems to look forward, as also in "After Apple-Picking," to the final rest that succeeds all engagements with reality.

Elsewhere, these same thematic relationships are made explicit. Thus, in "The Investment," a married couple is seen as trying to unite "potatoes" with "piano and new paint," in order to "get some color and music out of life." In "Two Tramps in Mud Time," the speaker's happiness consists in the uniting of the task of chopping wood (certified as practically necessary by the thought of frosty nights yet to come) with a perceptive look at a bluebird and a sensuous delight in the limber play of his own muscles.

Toward the end of the poem there is a burst of moralizing leading off with a manifesto couched in heavily Latinate and abstract language:

> But yield who will to their separation,
> My object in living is to unite
> My avocation and my vocation

In this final stanza, the two dimensions are named outright as *avocation* and *vocation*, *love* and *need*, *play* and *work*, "Heaven and the future's sakes."

In "The Investment" and "Two Tramps in Mud Time," the saliency against the native backdrop of certain Romance and Latinate elements of diction—*extravagance*, *impulse*, *color*, and *music* in the former, *separation*, *object*, *unite*, *avocation*, and *vocation* in the latter—may well seem too obvious, their thematic role too pat to be interesting. Such words operate more subtly and satisfactorily in other poems to highlight an aesthetic or meditative turn in the speaker's train of thought: for example, *pale orchises* in "Mowing," *petals* and *passion* in "Putting in the Seed," *scented*, *stuff*, and the disregarded *mountain ranges* of "Out, Out—," and, in "Two Tramps" itself, *tenderly*, *plume*, *crystal*, and *vernal*. In responding to their particular expressiveness, most clearly perceptible where a native synonym (*love*, *rows* [of mountains], *softly*, *spring*) is available for comparison, the reader gains a heightened sense of the verbal texture of the poem.

Once the thematic pattern I have described is identified, it becomes possible to see a closely related pattern in what might be called "poems of observation" as opposed to the previously discussed "poems of the task." The "task" now takes the form of disciplined observation itself, a long close look at the object free of philosophical or emotional preconceptions, while the "imaginative dimension" appears as a moment of insight or understanding validated by the process of which it is the culmination. The two groups of poems have in common a single structural paradigm: a dramatized movement in which some saving grace of widening awareness at once builds on and transcends, in New Testament fashion, the limitations of an original point of view.

An adequate discussion of this related group of poems is not possible within the limits of this essay, but a few brief comments may serve to indicate the direction such a discussion would take. In "Hyla Brook," a scrupulously unsentimental account of how the farmer-poet's brook goes dry and drab in summer yields an insight into the nature of love, which, to be worthy of the name, must (as my earlier paraphrase had it) be based on the nature of the object in reality. In "The Oven Bird," the refusal to sentimentalize either the bird or the late summer season is equally insistent. Here the positive significance of the ending, despite the fact that it is phrased as a question, depends on an implicit identification of the dramatized train of thought with the act of writing poetry. Again, as in "Mowing," the associations of the verb *make* with the word *poetry* and its cognates are called into play. We note, too, that the question "what to make of a diminished thing" is *framed* by the bird, rather than merely *put* or *posed*—that is, he builds something around it. As with the bird, so with the poet, who is also traditionally a "singer." For him, the answer to the question is the poem itself. In "The Wood-Pile," too, despite the melancholy final cadence ending on the word *decay*, the motion of the plot is basically expansive and outward-reaching. The speaker's quest carries him from his initial consciousness of an oppressive, prison-like scene ("the view was all in lines / Straight up and down") to an act of imaginative identification with an unknown other man whose self-forgetfulness he sympathetically admires. The poem is a later version of "The Tuft of Flowers" in minor key.

The language of these poems has the same extremely low Romance-Latinate content that was found earlier in the "poems of the task," and the dramatic significance of this feature remains the same: in addition to expressing a descriptive subject matter drawn from country life, the diction implies a casual, unpretentious manner and a reluctance to perceive the subject in abstractive or qualitative terms. A significant proportion of the Romance-Latinate elements themselves, as in the earlier group, can be seen as "symptomatic" of a turn toward the analytical or aesthetic in the speaker's thought: *remember* in "Hyla Brook," *question* and *diminished* in "The Oven Bird," *paused, view, lines* in "The Wood-Pile." Some serve less obvious purposes; in "The Wood-Pile," *cord* (signifying a precise quantity), *measured,* and *clematis* add a nuance of "scientific" accuracy to the speaker's observations; in "Hyla Brook" the cluster *flourished, jewel* (in *jewel-weed*), and *foliage* functions ironically to imply qualities not actually present in the main subject, the brook. And some—*June, paper* in "Hyla Brook," *trunk, sound, past* in "The Oven Bird," *save, place, pile, carry* in "The Wood-Pile"—have no particular saliency, simply merging as additional items into the level of common diction represented by the native words which constitute over 90 percent of the poems.

In Frost's later volumes there occurs a perceptible shift toward a more elaborate and literary language, due in part to an increase in the number of poems in the satiric and discursive modes. Statistically, the Romance-Latinate component of Frost's later language falls less often to the low extreme represented by "Mending Wall" and others. But the insight into dramatic structure yielded by a study of the simple language of the early poems remains useful, if only as something that can be tried on to see if it will fit, and the "causes" or "significance" of the heavier load of Romance-Latinate language furnishes in itself a topic of potential interest. I must limit myself here to a discussion of one poem, "Directive" (originally published in *Steeple Bush* in 1947). "Directive" is notoriously opaque even as regards its verbal surface, while its deeper meaning has been the occasion of almost as much disagreement as discussion. The comparatively literary diction of the poem is reflected by successive Romance-Latinate percentiles, for the first 500 words, of 11, 20 (lines 12–24), 10, 7, and 15 (lines 48–59). (The poem contains 524 words in all.) It is also reflected by the perceptibly elevated quality of such words as *monolithic, serial ordeal, village cultures,* and *Grail.* Despite its enigmatic character and certain flaws of tone which I shall touch on in due course, "Directive" may well be, in Reuben Brower's words, "the major poem of Frost's later years."

Reading the opening sentence, we are immediately struck by its syntactic and rhetorical elaboration. The main clause is delayed until line 5, and is both preceded and followed by parallel constructions. In mode, the opening is literary rather than anecdotal, the first five lines being an expansion of the "once upon a time" or "long ago" formula used by tellers of old stories in invoking the dark backward and abysm of time. But it also contains a contradiction which may easily escape us on a first reading, for it says, not that long ago there *was,* but that long ago there *is.* Other contradictions follow as, in a series of riddling paradoxes, we are told of "a house that is no more a house / Upon a farm that is no more a farm / And in a town that is no more a town." The speaker now explicitly introduces himself as "a guide," one who, again paradoxically, "only has at heart your getting lost." As he proceeds to describe the landscape through which his directive is to take us, and especially as he dictates our actions after we have arrived, it becomes increasingly apparent that he has much in common with the narrators of the old epics and romances, poets who were not mere tale-tellers but repositories of historical knowledge and transmitters of ethical ideals. Any solemnity implied by such a role, however, is undercut by his casual manner and jocular tone. His remark "And there's a story in a book about it" (I take the "story" to be the account of the glacier which follows, as the colon at the end of the line would imply) might have assumed some such more pretentious form as "There exists a published account of the geological history of the locality." (According to *ODEE,* the words *story* and *history* are both Latinate, deriving ultimately from *historia,* but the more extensive phonetic change visible in *story* is a sign of its more colloquial status, earlier as now.) The monolithic ledges on the mountainside are humorously compared to bare knees sticking out of torn or worn pants left unmended, and the treatment of the personified Glacier, who, as he wielded his chisel, "braced his feet against the Arctic Pole," is whimsical.

If we take the riddling and contradictory character of the opening as a sign that it is a kind of test imposed on the reader by the poet, we will not be surprised to find that the journey in store for him is also a test—an initiation rite designed to elicit proof of courage—in which the "guide," while pretending to reassure, actually gives more and more cause for alarm. There is menace and a suggestion of the uncanny in the "coolness" that "haunts" the quarry-like road. The very name *Panther Mountain* implies the mountain lions that once inhabited the New England wilderness. The reader is told that he will be "watched" as if by hidden eyes, that there will be sudden "light rustle rushes" in the leaves. He is encouraged to make himself up "a cheering song"—that is, to whistle in the dark—but the comfortable notion that this was once "someone's road home from work" turns suddenly into the unsettling possibility of an apparition on the road just ahead. The speaker in these lines reminds us of Robert Frost the man in his irritating aspect of professional tease—the teacher who liked to challenge his students to figure out whether he was serious or "fooling." But the teasing manner is dropped once the reader arrives at the lost farm and prepares to receive the enlightenment traditionally following upon the ordeal of initiation. Any expectations of explicit moral counsel he may have, however, are disappointed. Rather, he is instructed in the enactment of a ritual: he must drink from "a brook that was the water of the house" from "a broken drinking goblet" stolen by his guide from "the children's house of make believe, / Some shattered dishes underneath a pine."

The meaning of this ritual must be inferred in part from a series of images, present throughout the poem, in which natural processes of attrition and obliteration—including, on a grand scale, the geological processes embodied in the glacier—are seen as working against, and eventually defeating, man's efforts to maintain life in an inhospitable setting—a favorite subject of Frost's. The first such image is that of the gravestone sculpture "burned, dissolved, and broken off" by time and the weather. The distant past, which is the subject of the comparison, is called "a time made simple by the loss / Of detail," and here, too, the poet has planted a hidden meaning which can easily escape us. Ostensibly, he is making the standard comparison between the hyper-complexity of the present ("all this now too much for us," where *now* serves at once as adverb and noun) and the simplicity of a primitive past. But the past was not simple in the past; it has been "made simple" by the distance which separates us from it. The poem restores the lost details dissolved by this distant perspective, and these—the iron wagon wheels moving over rocky roads, the fields and apple orchards cleared in woods, the cellar holes and the houses built over them, the creaking buggy-loads of grain, together with the firkins, harness galls, and rising dough gratuitously invoked in comparisons—collectively represent the labor of establishing and maintaining a foothold in the wilderness: the hardships of the economic dimension of life and the courage and strength required to endure them. "This was no playhouse but a house in earnest." For this earnestness, the cold water of the brook that once supplied the house is an apt symbol.

But we have learned to look in Frost for the imaginative dimension without which labor is stultifying and for this another symbol is close at hand: the medicinal waters of the brook cannot be drunk except from the hidden goblet. Through its association with "the playhouse of the children,"the goblet is linked with the imagination (understated by Frost as "make believe") and a joy transcending harsh reality to which we are told we must sympathetically respond ("Weep for what little things could make them glad"). The two together—necessity and imagination, earnestness and joy, the water and the goblet containing it—make up the integrity or "whole-ness" which the act of drinking is said to bestow.

If, in the light of this interpretation, we look again at the language of the poem, it becomes clear that the comparatively high Romance-Latinate component of certain passages has its significance in relation to the character of the speaker, as compared with the speaker of "Mending Wall" and other early poems. Such words function to suggest, in a basically understated and casual style, the historical knowledge, the intellectual overview appropriate to the traditional bard-figure of poetic narrative. They include *sculpture, monolithic, enormous, Glacier, Arctic Pole, serial, inexperience, and cultures*—all Latinate except for *Glacier* (Romance) and *monolithic* (a French borrowing from Greek). To these should be added a group of words whose presence in the poem has frequently been noted, and which associate the speaker specifically with the narrators of the chivalric romances: *adventure, goblet, haunt,* and *Grail,* all Romance. (*Spell* and *ordeal,* which serve the same purpose, are of native derivation.)

But there is also a sort of allusiveness in the language of the poem which involves native rather than Romance or Latinate diction, and in recognizing this we are brought face to face with the problem posed by the speaker's explicit reference to the Gospel of Mark in the concluding lines.

The passage in question, as identified by Frost himself, is Mark 4:11–12, two verses which immediately follow the parable of the sowing of the seed on thorny and good ground:

> And he said unto them, Unto you it is given to know the mystery of the kingdom of God: but unto them that are without, all these things are done in parables:
>
> That seeing they may see, and not perceive; and hearing they may hear, and not understand; lest at any time they should be converted, and their sins should be forgiven them.

In addition to this overt reference, there are other more or less obvious allusions to the New Testament. The line "And if you're lost enough to find yourself" unmistakably (if colloquially) echoes Matthew 10:39: "He that findeth his life shall lose it: and he that loseth his life for my sake shall find it" (cf. Luke 17:33). Several critics have seen a connection between the importance of the children's playhouse in the concluding ritual and the emphasis in the gospels upon becoming as a little child, for example, in Matthew 18:3: "Except ye... become as little children, ye shall not enter into the kingdom of heaven" (cf. 19:14). Frost does not speak of "*little* children," but the Christian connotations of the adjective, as well as the paradoxical importance in Christian doctrine of the trivial and humble, seem implicitly present in the instruction to "weep for what little things could make them glad." (It is perhaps worth noting that references to "little ones" and "a cup of cold water" are found side by side in Matthew 10:42.) The word *water*, of course, has important associations in the New Testament with both physical and spiritual healing, that is, salvation, as in John 5:1–13 and Revelation 21:6; and so too does the word *whole* (Matthew 9:21–22, 14:36, etc.). These words form the same sort of allusive network I noted earlier in "Mending Wall"; they function similarly to elevate the style of certain passages of the poem, and they associate the speaker with the Christian tradition as well as with traditions of secular literature and learning.

The passage in Mark identifying the "wrong ones," those who will not be able to find the goblet, makes it clear that the salvation promised at the end of the poem is available only to those who understand what is said in "parables." If by a parable we mean a story in which things and actions are to be interpreted symbolically, differing from allegory not so much in the formal relationship between literal and symbolic as in the homely and everyday character of its subject matter and its emphasis upon the moral qualities of human action, then poems like "Mending Wall," "Mowing," "Hyla Brook," and others discussed above are, precisely, parables. So too

is the conclusion of "Directive." Only if we understand the symbolic significance of the ritual will we receive its saving moral message: only in the
imagination capable of understanding these symbols is the "good ground"
on which the message will bear fruit. Yet the message itself, it must be
insisted, is not Christian. The revelation the poem brings is moral rather
than supernatural; its source is not a divine incarnation but a secular figure,
the poet, who, although his garments may resemble the priest's, belongs to
the realm of human experience and memory. Despite his exploitation of the
Christian tradition in the structure, symbolism, and language of his poems,
the supreme bearer of spiritual enlightenment in our time, for Frost, was
poetry itself. The last line of "Directive," as S. P. C. Duvall has pointed
out, is reminiscent of the poet's famous definition of poetry as "a momentary
stay against confusion."

In setting himself up as the exclusive "guide" ("And put a sign up
CLOSED to all but me") to a truth he has hedged about with verbal and
symbolic obscurities, and in proceeding to imply that only those who can
interpret this poetically mediated truth are worthy to be saved, Frost, one
may well think, has his nerve. The teasing and testing, the archness and
complacent whimsy, will always alienate a certain number of readers, and
long familiarity will not render them any less irritating. But though "Directive" is flawed in part by the arch-avuncular pose of the elderly Frost,
it is not seriously damaged. The ideal it upholds—the encompassing of
Puritanical grimness and strength by a saving joy and imagination—is powerful and viable in this as in the other poems which make up Frost's New
Testament. And, in "Directive" particularly, we must admire the brilliance
with which so great a range of resources—rural Americana, American-style
humorous understatement, legend, history and fairy tale, the literary past,
the chivalric and Christian traditions—has been drawn upon and forged
into a stylistic whole. Here, as in all Frost's best poems, what is literary
and elevated seems not to impose itself upon, but to rise naturally from,
basic simplicity—the everyday things of country life, lucidly and concretely
rendered in common language—which is Frost's primary and most memorable poetic world.

SYDNEY LEA

From Sublime to Rigamarole:
Relations of Frost to
Wordsworth

I. HEIRS AND HEIRLESSNESS

Given their mutual attraction to nature, pastoral, and ballad, it is un-surprising that Robert Frost saw in Wordsworth a primary influence. His famous claim that *North of Boston* "dropped to an everyday level of diction that even Wordsworth kept above" shows that influence; it also shows the competitive stance which Frost always adopted toward this ancestor. Con-sider the turns of a lengthy speech—the "Tribute to Wordsworth" given at Cornell University's 1950 symposium commemorating the centennial of Wordsworth's death. Frost starts by noticing the brevity of Wordsworth's major period, but quickly protests, "I'm not here to take away from him at all." Yet he persistently deflects attention from Wordsworth, either by digression (protracted quotations from other poets) or by diffusing Wordsworth's prominence in the occasion, let alone in poetic tradition: "People ask me what I read. Why, I read Shakespeare, and I read Words-worth, and I read almost anything." The process of refocussing is gener-ally ironic or left-handed: "But I haven't by dislike or distaste eliminated much of Wordsworth. Most of it will do very well."

The speech thus establishes a triple affective structure: distraction from Wordsworth, doubt about his accomplishment (his "tone . . . of Simple Si-mon," his "insipidity," his "banal" quality), and final, partial qualification of doubt:

From *Studies in Romanticism* 19, no. 1 (Spring 1980). ©1980 by the Trustees of Boston University.

85

> I think that's the essential Wordsworth. That lovely banality and that penetration that goes with it. It goes right down into the soul of man, and always, there'll be one line that's just as penetrating as anything anybody ever wrote.

Of course, the ordering of components in that structure is variable:

> Let's say one of Wordsworth's. (I don't want to act as if the only poet I didn't know was Wordsworth, after I've come here to celebrate him.) You know what I'd read you if I could? I'd read "Michael." That I've always admired very, very much, but it's too long, and as I looked at it this afternoon . . . I found it went on page after page. I'd forgotten that. It had made a better impression on me than that.

What, then, was the influence Frost felt? Simply, not a so-called Romantic one; indeed, Frost comes closest to direct tribute in remarks on "Ode to Duty," in which Wordsworth discards his own "Romanticism." It is this disenchanted poet who informs Frost's work, but Frost (with real acuteness) had heard the disenchanted voice even in the assured poetry of Wordsworth's egotistical sublime. In this essay I will try to read Wordsworth's poems as Frost did, for Frost's canon may be seen as a purgation of Wordsworth's, "dropping" below his predecessor's in more than stylistic ways, dispelling even the vestigial illusions, as Frost views them, of the chastened Wordsworth. As we shall see, it displaces Imagination with *Fancy* (or "Yankee" skepticism: unwillingness to suspend disbelief, wit or reason). Pastoral retreat concomitantly collapses into stingy timbered-land, belief in a possible sublime into stubborn earthiness, poem as redemption into poem as "rigamarole."

If Frost scoured his ancestor's legacy, the gesture might have hurt Wordsworth but probably not have surprised him. Though, like any poet, the latter was much concerned with the very matter of legacy, major poems of the Great Decade suggest something more like obsession. In "Lines Composed a Few Miles Above Tintern Abbey," for example, the writer revisits a place connected with "the soul / Of all [his] moral being" in order to assure himself "That in this moment there is life and food / For future years"; but it is his sister who signals hope even beyond those years, for she will recall her brother's "exhortations" (the climactic turns of the poem itself) and provide him with at least a serial immortality.

Yet a kind of undertone throughout the poem bespeaks the writer's worry lest his reader assume a Frostian skepticism towards its assertions.

Here, the word "exhortations" betrays unease behind Wordsworth's "cheerful faith" in imaginative legacy. We read in it an inkling of the self-subduing gestures of reaction, later poems like "Ode to Duty" or "Elegiac Stanzas" which at once validate the unease and seek support in acceptance and endurance.

Beginning with his forefather's belatedly acquired clarity, Frost proceeded often to witticize it. Indeed, we can ourselves fancifully construe certain Frost lyrics as disenchantedly Wordsworthian, as ironic "replies" to pieces like "Tintern Abbey" which open onto faith in posterity:

Closed for Good

Much as I own I owe
The passers of the past
Because their to and fro
Has cut this road to last,
I owe them more today
Because they've gone away

And come not back with steed
And chariot to chide
My slowness with their speed
And scare me to one side.
They have found other scenes
For haste and other means.

They leave the road to me
To walk in saying naught
Perhaps but to a tree
Inaudibly in thought,
"From you the road receives
A priming coat of leaves.

"And soon for lack of sun
The prospects are in white
It shall be further done,
But with a coat so light
The shape of leaves will show
Beneath the brush of snow."

And so on into winter
Till even I have ceased

To come as a foot printer,
And only some slight beast
So mousy or so foxy
Shall print there as my proxy.

The first four lines want only end-stopping to be a complete, alternately-rhymed quatrain; we read them so in passing, and momentarily suppose a confession of total debt: the poet "owes" all he "owns" to pioneers. But the end of the stanza corrects the misreading its introduction invites. Frost's gratitude is that they have "gone away" and left for him a clearing. ("Closed for Good," aptly, would at last appear in *In the Clearing*.) Given the "steeds" and "chariots" in the next stanza, we must strain to assume that Frost refers only to departed farmers; yet we needn't choose, for the poem merges literal and literary pathbreakers (note the play on "leaves" and "prints" throughout). Frost here turns *all* his predecessors into epic figures. But this merely prepares us for further irony, for disenchanted commentary as in "Tintern Abbey": "They have found other scenes / For haste and other means." Like the poem at large, these amount to vacancy and silence. Frost dismisses the premise of Wordsworth's "cheerful faith," that some generous and perpetual force linking mind and nature survives in a poem's accomplishment.

For the world Frost enters is miserly: earlier passers have bequeathed him only this slight road "To walk in saying naught." The quoted but inaudible address to a tree, then, in stanzas three and four constitutes mute poem-within-poem (like Wordsworth's address to his sister), but sets terms of natural perception contradictory to those of "Tintern Abbey." "From you," says Frost, "the road receives / A priming coat of leaves." With nature's priming gesture, Wordsworth blends his own gesture; for unlike Frost's exclusively visual and silent world, Wordsworth's scene involves the "eye and ear,—both what they half create / And what perceive." While "the light of setting suns" was for Wordsworth part of a sober but sustaining "motion and a spirit, that impels / All thinking things, all objects of all thought," Frost finds a grimmer impulse in nature:

"And soon for lack of sun
The prospects are in white
It shall be further done,
But with a coat so light
The shape of leaves will show
Beneath the brush of snow."

The inner Frost poem is also a poem of inner frost. Autumnal, conscious of its transitoriness, it does not blend with, but reflects the gathering cold of its natural scene. Yet even the reflection is but half successful, for the poet's "leaves" are like nature's only in falling, not in the prospect of return. The final stanza, a meditation on the interstitial lyric, shows that nature, however gradually, impels the assays of this "foot printer" (a canny trope for *poet*) back to the status of the blank page. Even if we ignore Frost's pun on heirlessness ("lack of sun"), the tough wit of his ending implies his poetic fate: winter will erase his "prints" and "only some slight beast... / Shall print there as [his] proxy." Frost substitutes stark declaration for exhortation, lacking the consolation of human continuity embodied in Wordsworth's Dorothy.

The degeneracy of Frost's actual (and un-Wordsworthian) context—the clearings reverted to popple and hardhack—drives home the lessons of "Closed for Good." One of his letters appropriately suggested this flinty lyric as "a new end piece symbolically" for the 1949 reissue of *North of Boston*. We know that volume's announcement of competition with Wordsworth, so that if there is self-irony in the letter when Frost pledges also "to write a small preface to go desperately down to posterity with," there may too be wry reference to the last great writer of prefaces.

And of "desperate" ones, if we adopt a Frostian view: consider the 1800 Preface to *Lyrical Ballads*, which seeks among other things to justify the use of country-language as "a more permanent, and a far more philosophical" mode than that of the contemporary polite world, or of passers past. Even idealizing Frost's "pastoral" agenda, we cannot imagine him speaking so. Yet Wordsworth's very style, apologetic and circumlocutory, suggests that Wordsworth was hard put to overcome Frostian skepticism not only in his readers but also perhaps in himself. It is not, for example, he who is anxious to defend the permanent relevance of his language or his material, but

> Several of my Friends are anxious for the success of these Poems, from a belief, that, if the views with which they were composed were indeed realised, a class of Poetry would be produced, well adapted to interest mankind permanently, and not unimportant in the quality, and in the multiplicity of its moral relations.

Wordsworth does not claim personal success. But if someone were to achieve his aims, pleasure "would be produced"; this is not to say obviously important pleasure, but "not unimportant." And so on. Wordsworth's claim is for the potential and not actual value of his volume, its status as the model of a model. Because it *promises* so much, friends "have advised me to prefix a systematic defense of the theory upon which the Poems were written":

> But I was unwilling to undertake the task, knowing that on the occasion, the Reader would look coldly upon my arguments, since I might be suspected of having been principally influenced by the selfish and foolish hope of *reasoning* him into an approbation of these particular Poems.

Does Wordsworth's diffidence about the particular poems arise from fear that their prospects will ultimately be closed for good? Such an assumption would lead to even soberer revision of "Tintern Abbey," which often suggests a cognate indirection:

> If this
> Be but a vain belief, yet oh! how oft—
> In darkness and amid the many shapes
> Of joyless daylight; when the fretful stir
> Unprofitable, and the fever of the world,
> Have hung upon the beatings of my heart—
> How oft, in spirit, have I turned to thee!
> O sylvan Wye, thou wanderer thro' the woods,
> How often has my spirit turned to thee!
>   (ll. 49–57)

Turnings and re-turnings of the mind—repetitive, *often*—counter the momentary fear of vanity. Yet Frost, whose sense of the world implies debilitatingly abrupt progression without return, would construe such palliative wandering as self-delusion or masked apology.

The passage just quoted follows the famous one "in which the burthen of the mystery,/In which the heavy and the weary weight/Of all this unintelligible world / Is lightened" and, "almost suspended," "we see into the life of things." The blankness of "Closed for Good" represents Frost's general wariness of such lightening and penetration. Even in "Birches," where a dual mental movement, back in time and upward from life's "burthen," seems at one point to recall "Tintern Abbey," Frost's unwillingness to rise through imagination to "Intellectual Love" (*The Prelude* IV.207) reveals itself in the end:

> So was I once myself a swinger of birches.
> And so I dream of going back to be.

> It's when I'm weary of considerations,
> And life is too much like a pathless wood
> Where your face tickles and burns with the cobwebs
> Broken across it, and one eye is weeping
> From a twig's having lashed across it open.
> I'd like to get away from earth awhile.

Yet Frost checks his dream of being "almost suspended":

> And then come back to it and begin over.
> May no fate willfully misunderstand me
> And half grant what I wish and snatch me away
> Not to return. Earth's the right place for love:
> I don't know where it's likely to go better.

The "weariness" comes, in this beautiful passage and the one it echoes, from life in the fragmented adult world. Frost refrains here from urbanizing this malaise, yet the yearning in either poem is a pastoral one for uncluttered zones beyond confusion. "The world is too much with us," says a Wordsworth sonnet which adumbrates a pastoral remedy as does Frost's "New Hampshire": " 'Me for the hills where I don't have to choose.' " For both poets the northern return is a regression to simplified decisions and values.

However, the simplification does not console Frost as it does Wordsworth, as another juxtaposition—"Lines Written in Early Spring" and Frost's "Spring Pools"—will attest. The former stresses a blending intrinsic to the natural scene:

> I heard a thousand blended notes,
> While in a grove I sate reclined,
> In that sweet mood when pleasant thoughts
> Bring sad thoughts to the mind.
>
> To her fair works did Nature link
> The human soul that through me ran;
> And much it grieved my heart to think
> What man has made of man.
>
> Through primrose tufts, in that green bower,
> The periwinkle trailed its wreaths;
> And 'tis my faith that every flower
> Enjoys the air it breathes.

The birds around me hopped and played.
Their thoughts I cannot measure,
But the least motion that they made,
It seemed a thrill of pleasure.

The budding twigs spread out their fan,
To catch the breezy air;
And I must think, do all I can,
That there was pleasure there.
If this belief from Heaven be sent,
If such be Nature's holy plan,
Have I not reason to lament
What man has made of man?

The lyric implies the conviction, elaborately voiced in longer poems, that nature as well as man delights in harmony, yet shows that the conviction can never empirically be validated. Hence, the illogical leaps in all stanzas: the periwinkles bloom, "*and* 'tis my faith that every flower / Enjoys the air it breathes"; the musical birds have thoughts immeasurable, and their sporting "*seemed* a thrill of pleasure." Or, most odd, the twigs catch the breeze, "And I must think, do all I can, / That there was pleasure there." That first line, apparently a groping for rhyme, is actually a prosodical protest of faith against the fear that natural reciprocity may only be a fancy, or what is the same, only seemingly a signal of pleasure. The fear is, if at all, only partly overcome in the ballad, which ends quite conditionally: "If this belief from Heaven be sent, / If such be Nature's holy plan,..." Wordsworth would have his belief in pleasure-through-reciprocity attain the status of imaginative myth, but cannot here assert that status.

He has at the outset described *himself* illogically as being in that "sweet mood" which causes sadness: the very business of feeling so good raises the spectre of opposite feeling, pleasure in harmony the spectre of disharmony, and vernal vision the spectre of winter. He laments "what man has made of man," which is, of course, pastoral reaction against industrialism and the mentality spawned by it, but also against "man" as adult, victim/perpetrator of complexity and fragmentation as opposed to the fullness and simplicity of seedtime. Wordsworth's pastoral tendency is always linked with nature (whose objects are themselves interfusing); if the adult poet cannot link the human soul to natural pleasure, he will have no pastoral— or will be grimly aware of the *past* in "pastoral," the fallacy in what we have come to call pathetic fallacy. Written as a companion piece to "To My Sister," moreover, "Early Spring" is part of the legacy which Wordsworth extends to us through his exhortations to Dorothy: a legacy, he knows, of disenchantment if indeed his faith proves fanciful.

In spite of his lyric's anguish and lamentation, though, Wordsworth at least hopes for a possible association of natural and human renewals, unlike Frost in his spring meditation:

Spring Pools

These pools that, though in forests, still reflect
The total sky almost without defect,
And like the flowers beside them, chill and shiver,
Will like the flowers beside them soon be gone,
And yet not out by any brook or river,
But up by roots to bring dark foliage on.

The trees that have it in their pent-up buds
To darken nature and be summer woods—
Let them think twice before they use their powers
To blot out and drink up and sweep away
These flowery waters and these watery flowers
From snow that melted only yesterday.

Frost's poem also invites a view of natural harmony, if only the most tenuous kind (note the subordination of the opening stanza which qualifies that harmony as it announces it); yet its speaker—far less active than Wordsworth's—does not project the connection of landscape and sky beyond the moment. Indeed, he has no power to do so, for all agency is nature's: nature appears to be "souled" (may even "think twice"), but is also latently violent (note the "pent-up buds" like caged beasts). Immediately as she brightens, teasing us with synthesis "almost without defect," she darkens, and this is partly because of *contest* among the objects of nature.

Wordsworth, perhaps feeling the chill of such bleak progression and strife, still does "all he can" to contravene it, so that the threat of disharmony in the scene occurs to us only as inference from his overprotest. Nothing rises up from Frost's landscape to motivate such compensatory effort. The poet eschews lament, because he sees the absoluteness of change and degeneration, the futility of complaint.

Of course the pools themselves rise up, "But up by roots to bring dark foliage on." This is not the upward movement of Wordsworth's poem (grove-flowers-birds-trees-air and finally "Heaven"), which suggests sublimation, but an upwardness to obliteration: the quick future will "blot out and drink up and sweep away" the scene that merges flower, water and sky.

Wordsworth, simply, fears vacancy; Frost assumes it, for instants of natural fullness are so fleeting as to be delusory, and human achievement is almost equally so. The Frost of "Spring Pools" remains an observer rather than a rhetorician because, as his scene persuades him, it is feckless to exhort the void. One needs an heir to supply a legacy: poetic stasis (as in "Closed for Good") is, like natural stasis, momentary.

Consider poems in which Frost imagines *himself* as the heir to an artist; his befuddlement in that role shows how foreign are an artifact's genesis and context to its observers, how insufficient therefore art as monument. The stone-cutter of "To an Ancient," for example, has "two claims to immortality": "You made the eolith, you grew the bone." Rather than consolation (*ars longa, vita brevis*), Frost oddly offers "the second"—the bone—as "more peculiarly your own, / And likely to have been enough alone." Enough for what, for immortality? Surely not, but if even bodily traces outlast man's making, Wordsworth's faith is in danger of ceding to despair. The interrogatives of Frost's final stanza may moot the despair, but do not cancel its threat:

> You make me ask if I would go to time
> Would I gain anything by using rhyme?
> Or aren't the bones enough I live to lime?

Frost says in "A Missive Missile" (as so often, he puns, and doubly stresses *miss*ing) that "Someone in ancient Mas d'Azil / Once took a little pebble wheel / And dotted it with red for me, / And sent it to me years and years." He then fancies that

> his ghost is standing by
> Importunate to give the hint
> And be successfully conveyed.
> How anyone can fail to see
> Where perfectly in form and tint
> The metaphor, the symbol lies!
> Why will I not analogize?
> (I do too much in some men's eyes.)
> Oh, slow uncomprehending me,
> Enough to make a spirit moan
> Or rustle in a bush or tree.
> I have the ocher-written flint,
> The two dots and the ripple line.

> The meaning of it is unknown,
> Or else I fear entirely mine.

Frost himself, of course, suffers several ironies here. A poet's skepticism of art is necessarily self-skepticism, and the poem's jogging tetrameter suggests inconsequence. Moreover, the poet, if anything overly given to metaphor and analogy, misses the meaning of this missile sent over time; who then will grasp it? The stone seems to ask Frost for an analogy between primitive and modern makers, perhaps as deathless figures. But he represses this response, which would signal the sublimely egotistical postulation of "the noble living and the noble dead" (*The Prelude* XI. 395). Frost's chiding of himself, like that of "Closed for Good," for slowness and incomprehension is misleading, for he knows that any "comprehension" would be self-fabricated. As Wordsworth, in temporary disillusionment about the lives and legacies of earlier poets, said: "By our own spirits are we deified." Compare Frost's equally double-edged line: "The metaphor, the symbol lies!" Distortion and self-deception are inevitable, for

> Far as we aim our signs to reach,
> Far as we often make them reach,
> Across the soul-from soul abyss,
> There is an aeon-limit set
> Beyond which they are doomed to miss.
> Two souls may be too widely met.
> That sad-with-distance river beach
> With mortal longing may beseech;
> It cannot speak as far as this.

Frost, of course, implies that the artifact's obscurity is a product of its antiquity; but this is to quibble. The process whereby soul and soul lapse into incommunication may indeed be long, but is inevitable. If the message wrought in stone is cloudy, then what, our incurable punster might ask, are words worth?

II. FROM PASTORAL SUBLIME TO RIGAMAROLE

Still we must deal with equivalently playful yet far tenderer work like "Directive," a poem which actually accepts a legacy and proffers one, thereby pointedly recalling Wordsworth's "Michael." Like so many of Wordsworth's poems, "Michael" is motivated by the search for landscape to serve "as a kind of permanent rallying point for [the] domestic feelings,

as a tablet upon which they are written which makes them objects of memory
in a thousand instances when they should otherwise be forgotten."

The livelihood of Wordsworth's shepherd thus has a kind of imme-
morial quality. His cottage, for example, is dignified by being called THE
EVENING STAR, as if constellated in some mythic order, which the curious
ritualism of this poem in fact implies:

> in a later time, ere yet the Boy
> Had put on boy's attire, did Michael love,
> Albeit of a stern, unbending mind,
> To have the Young-one in his sight, when he
> Wrought in the field, or on his shepherd's stool
> Sate with a fettered sheep before him stretched
> Under the large old oak, that near his door
> Stood single, and, from matchless depth of
>   shade,
> Chosen for the Shearer's covert from the sun,
> Thence in our rustic dialect was called
> THE CLIPPING TREE, a name which yet it bears.
> There, while they two were sitting in the shade,
> With others round them, earnest all and blithe,
> Would Michael exercise his heart with looks
> Of fond correction and reproof bestowed
> Upon the Child, if he disturbed the sheep.
>   (ll. 159–74)

In spite of fondness, Michael will not countenance disruption of this literal
pastoral mode: "correction" of the boy is essential to his initiation into that
mode, whose sacredness is betokened, for example, by the shrine-like CLIP-
PING TREE.

The pathos of "Michael" lies above all in the dissolution of ritualized
land and relation to land—ultimately THE EVENING STAR is gone and THE
CLIPPING TREE remains as anomaly in a transformed countryside. The search
for permanence reveals itself as illusion, save that Wordsworth claims to
have turned his very narrative into testimony to timeless pastoral values.
The poet accepts the legacy which the son has refused, and that acceptance
proves a saving grace against the degenerative drift of history.

Defending "Directive" against the interpretation which insists on its
"clear and disenchanted perception," David Sanders sees a Wordsworthian
gesture on Frost's part: the poet turns "make-believe ritual into a ritual
make-believe that carries the poem to its denouement." But Frost's "ritual

make-believe" is precisely *founded* on disenchanted clarity of view. Not to see this is to idealize; for example:

> The handing down of the vessel to the children, to the poet, and finally to us, suggests how life renews itself imaginatively *as* it does so physically.... As our salvation depends on him, so his survival depends on us. If the poem is necessary for him to save us, we are necessary if the poem shall save him.

This reading attributes a positive stance towards imaginative legacy to one deeply skeptical on that issue; its moral applies more obviously to the source-poem, "Michael," which does unironically offer a salvational scheme: to excite

> Profitable sympathies in many kind and good hearts, and ... in some small degree enlarge our feelings of reverence for our species, and our knowledge of human nature.... I thought, at a time when these feelings are sapped in so many ways, that ["Michael" and "The Brothers"] might cooperate, however feebly.

But in "Directive," according to its author, "The poet is not offering any general salvation.... In the midst of this now too much for us he tells everyone to go back ... to whatever source they have."

Salvation depends not on the poet but on ourselves: it is, moreover, a provisional fiction which tomorrow will undo. Frost sees as much in the landscape. It took literally centuries for the English northcountry to reach the pass lamented in "Michael"—

> The Cottage which was named THE EVENING STAR
> Is gone—the ploughshare has been through the ground
> On which it stood; great changes have been wrought
> In all the neighbourhood: yet the oak is left
> That grew beside their door; and the remains
> Of the unfinished Sheep-fold may be seen
> Beside the boisterous brook of Greenhead Ghyll—
> (ll. 476–82)

but north of Boston, beside the waters of "Directive," this process has been effected in less than a hundred years: the shepherds built their stone fences, and were destroyed by the Australian and Southwestern mutton industry; next, the dirt farmers passed their ploughshares through the ground, exposing the granite ribs that forced them off it; then the timberers cut down the pine and oak:

> As for the woods' excitement over you
> That sends light rustle rushes to their leaves,
> Charge that to upstart inexperience.
> Where were they all not twenty years ago?

The pastoral clearings have gone back to scrub growth and the whips of steeple bush that give the volume in which "Directive" appears its name. The leavings of pastors past do not make for lasting vision:

> Back in a time made simple by the loss
> Of detail, burned, dissolved, and broken off
> Like graveyard marble sculpture in the weather,
> There is a house that is no more a house
> Upon a farm that is no more a farm
> And in a town that is no more a town.
> The road there, if you'll let a guide direct you
> Who only has at heart your getting lost,
> May seem as if it should have been a quarry—
> Great monolithic knees the former town
> Long since gave up pretense of keeping covered.
> And there's a story in a book about it:
> Besides the wear of iron wagon wheels
> The ledges show lines ruled southeast-northwest,
> The chisel work of an enormous glacier
> That braced his feet against the Arctic Pole.

Both Wordsworth and Frost guide us up an uncouth road and back to a story, urging us to lose our complicated selves and to find truer ones. But there is a characteristically mischievous ring in Frost's invitation, as if the retreat in time freed us for whimsy rather than Wordsworthian moral vigor. Frost's "tale" never gets beyond the deliberately vague and playful hints of his opening lines, while Wordsworth reconstructs a long and serious story:

> It was the first
> Of those domestic tales that spake to me
> Of Shepherds, dwellers in the valleys, men
> Whom I already loved;
>
> .   .   .   .
>
> And hence this Tale, while I was yet a Boy
> Careless of books, yet having felt the power
> Of Nature, by the gentle agency

Of natural objects, led me on to feel
For passions that were not my own, and think
(At random and imperfectly indeed)
On man, the heart of man, and human life.

(ll. 21–33)

Much has to do with the poets' divergent views of nature. Frost stresses the bluntness of her "simplifying" (note the brute monosyllables, the harsh descriptives, the chill in the passage just cited). She is both gentle agent and inspiration to Wordsworth, and having felt her influence as both, Wordsworth confidently assumes a similar effect on his characters, especially Michael:

Those fields, those hills—what could they less? had laid
Strong hold on his affections, were to him
A pleasurable feeling of blind love,
The pleasure that there is in life itself.

(ll. 74–77)

Frost, eyes wide open, climbs his road as a stranger to such pastoralism (if ever it existed), skeptical of all "stories"—"in a book" or not—concerning it. "Directive" remains inchoate narrative, because the poet has not invented as he urges us to do:

Make yourself up a cheering song of how
Someone's road home from work this once was,
Who may be just ahead of you on foot
Or creaking with a buggy load of grain.
The height of the adventure is the height
Of country where two village cultures faded
Into each other. Both of them are lost.
And if you're lost enough to find yourself
By now, pull in your ladder road behind you
And put a sign up CLOSED to all but me.
Then make yourself at home. The only field
Now left's no bigger than a harness gall.
First there's the children's house of make-believe,
Some shattered dishes underneath a pine,
The playthings in the playhouse of the children.
Weep for what little things could make them glad.

Here is an instance of the peculiar Frostian tenderness which Wordsworth could never have managed, partly because he sought the broad vision and partly because his countryfolk, though threatened, still lived; they had not suffered a "loss of detail," for they had not in his view ever attained to complexity. Frost's emphasis on fading and indistinctness signals not interfusion (nor the blindness of love) but ruin brought on by mean climate and pinched nature. Archaic cultures have so melted into one another that the poet coaxes us to spin a make-believe story (an ellipsis for *fanciful history*). He invites us—half-jocularly, half-wistfully—to indulge our powers of feigning: in the words of Wordsworth's collaborator on *Lyrical Ballads* (as they appear by happy accident in "Frost at Midnight") to "make a Toy of Thought."

It is worth lingering momentarily with Coleridge, especially his recollection of Wordsworth's role in the 1798 volume:

> ...subjects were to be chosen from ordinary life; the characters and incidents were to be such, as will be found in every village and its vicinity, where there is a meditative and feeling mind to seek after them, or to notice them, when they present themselves....
>
> Mr. Wordsworth ... was to propose to himself as his object, to give the charm of novelty to things of every day, and to excite a feeling analogous to the supernatural, by awakening the mind's attention from the lethargy of custom, and directing it to the loveliness and the wonders of the world before us.

Coleridge's language reminds us of the eighteenth- and nineteenth-century controversy over sublime and beautiful, and limns his friend's relation to that controversy. Wordsworth's Imagination ("meditative and feeling mind") will *conflate* beautiful ("loveliness") and sublime ("wonders"). Indeed, Wordsworth will defamiliarize the landscape by imbuing the commonplaces of low and rustic life with an awesomeness heretofore reserved for epic or romance. Hence in "Michael," despite its "low" occasion, Wordsworth is unself-conscious about ritualism and straightforward in echoing Scripture, because he feels his naturalist program can arouse sensations akin to the supernatural. In "Directive," ritual has degenerated into whimsical make-believe, the Scriptural allusions at the end are deliberately near-facetious, the Grail of romance is a shattered plaything, and other romance or supernatural elements—the "eye pairs out of forty firkins," for example— are dismissed as upstarts. There are no characters or incidents besides the nameless ones which Frost fancifully calls up, a fact which shows the priority of his will in making the poem. Wordsworth, as Coleridge notes, is indifferent about priority: in his abundant world, the mind can either "seek after" fit matter for his song, or merely "notice" it, like mild revelation.

However arrived at, the loftiness of Wordsworth's concerns accounts for the urgency of his narrative, which seeks to purge our lethargy and to reveal in pastoral life a holy energy. Consider the title-character:

> in his shepherd's calling he was prompt
> And watchful more than ordinary men.
> Hence had he learned the meaning of all winds,
> Of blasts of every tone; and oftentimes,
> When others heeded not, he heard the South
> Make subterraneous music
>
> . . . .
>
> the storm, that drives
> The traveller to a shelter, summoned him
> Up to the mountains: he had been alone
> Amid the heart of many thousand mists,
> That came to him, and left him, on the heights.
>
> (ll. 46–60)

Michael's calling is to elevation and revelation. Coleridge's sense of Wordsworth shows its accuracy as this lowly figure, surrounded by the stormy wind and underworldly music, visits and is visited on the heights, in short as he participates in the very sublime whose language the poet uses here and in such famous passages as *The Prelude* VI and XIV. A rising mountain mist blurs or extinguishes mere sight, and we await a manifestation of the invisible world. Yet, as Coleridge observed, we cannot finally leave things of every day: vision remains nascent, "something ever more about to be," or, in the words of Thomas Weiskel:

> In the egotistical sublime the two ... poles of sensible nature and eschatological destination collapse inward and become "habitual" attributes of ... Imagination—a totalizing consciousness whose medium is sense but whose power is transcendent. Apocalypse becomes immanent; the sublime, a daily habit.

This habitual sublime is part of Wordsworth's crusade against loss and discontinuity, dissipating separations of numinous and actual, generous childhood and ironic adulthood, rendering phenomenological categories of high and low less stark, showing the distinction between "loveliness" and "wonder" to be no longer distinctive.

The effects of such revised sublimity are seen, for example, in Wordsworth's language, which commandeers for common speech the rhetorical
energy of the sublime, purging its turgid archaisms but retaining a "height"
appropriate to the lofty region which attracts the poet—and to his exalted
mission for pastoral.

Frost's subsequent purgation of Wordsworth is impelled by the most
elementary differences in world-view. We have sensed his skepticism of
Wordsworthian "blending"; as he says in a speech on Emerson, the great
native Romantic, "a melancholy dualism is the only soundness." Frost must
inevitably sunder the fusion of low pastoral and sublime *hypsos*: "The height
of the adventure is the height / Of country where two village cultures faded."
They faded as a star will fade from morning's heaven: Frost's clear daylight
vision *desublimates* his context, whereas Wordsworth can poetically reset
an EVENING STAR that has literally vanished.

We have seen that the speakers of "Michael" and "Directive" share
guide's roles, but our reading should be guided by differences in tone:
Wordsworth's call to "courage! for around that boisterous brook / The
mountains have all opened out themselves," as opposed to Frost's exhortation to privacy, find your *self* and *close* the road. The broad declamation
of "Michael" disappears from the later poem. It is, after all, a "boisterous"
watershed that Wordsworth traces; Frost's is "too lofty and original to
rage"; but this is part of make-believe, for nothing of loftiness is evident in
the rest of the poem, which also dramatizes the perils of originality. Frost
feigns a power in his necessarily lowered voice and diminished scene which
they do not have.

Let us, for a moment, pursue this digression on the waters by a con-
sideration of Frost's earlier "Hyla Brook" and Wordsworth's hymn to Imagination in *The Prelude* VI. 592–616, relating them as we did "Closed for
Good" and "Tintern Abbey." The passage from *The Prelude* runs a familiar
course. Imagination signals itself in mist and rises toward supra-natural
destiny; then the passage re-fuses (and refuses) the separateness of destiny
and sense. The soul, elevated by imagination, is renaturalized,

> Strong in herself and in beatitude
> That hides her, like the mighty flood of Nile
> Poured from his font of Abyssinian clouds
> To fertilize the whole Egyptian plain.
>
> (ll.614–16)

Quickened, "soul" descends powerfully into landscape, imagination mark-
ing this movement as one of possible sublimity, of *creative* power. (Words-

worth borrows the ancient association of Abyssinia and Eden.) The passage's elision of dualism indeed exemplifies the egotistical sublime by fulfilling the ends of what Wordsworth early called his "high argument": to show the reciprocity of mind and external world, "and the creation (by no lower name / Can it be called) which they with blended might / Accomplish" (*The Recluse*, ll. 822–24).

The very imagery of "Hyla Brook"—which like "Closed for Good" puns on the act of poetic creation—provides its own commentary on the distance between the waters which Wordsworth and Frost look upon:

> By June our brook's run *out of song and speed.*
> Sought for much after that, it will be found
> Either to have gone *groping underground*
> (And taken with it all the Hyla breed
> That *shouted in the mist* a month ago,
> Like *ghost* of sleigh bells in a ghost of snow)—
> Or flourished and come up in jewelweed,
> *Weak foliage* that is blown upon and bent,
> Even against the way its waters went.
> Its bed is left a *faded paper sheet*
> Of dead leaves stuck together by the heat—
> *A brook to none but who remember long.*
> This as it will be seen is *other far*
> *Than with brooks taken otherwhere in song.*
> We love the things we love for *what they are.*
>
> (emphasis added)

The underground groping of the brook/poem's song is distant indeed from the subterraneous music which Michael hears from the height of land, and the distance of waters from waters implies that of Frost from Wordsworth's imaginative structure: the sublime falling into nature, from which imagination evokes it into the "permanent" status of the poem's "leaves" (which, if they come at all, constitute "weak foliage" for Frost).

The portrait of Michael cited a moment ago incorporates the components of the sublime—height, vapor, singing winds—because these insubstantials soften the edges of perception (the sharp sight at work in "Hyla Brook"). For Wordsworth's object is to liberate us from the despotic bodily eye, "to make," in the words of a more sympathetic successor, "the visible a little hard to see" (Wallace Stevens, "The Creations of Sound"). Wordsworth's commonplace sublime interfuses sensory and mental and natural: up and down, dark and light.

> Visionary power
> Attends the motions of the viewless winds,
> Embodied in the mystery of words:
> There darkness makes abode, and all the host
> Of shadowy things works endless changes,—there,
> As in a mansion like their proper home,
> Even forms and substances are circumfused
> By that transparent veil with light divine,
> And, through the turnings intricate of verse,
> Present themselves as objects recognised,
> In flashes, and with glory not their own.
> *(Prelude* V. 595–605)

As the imagination tends to sublimity, the influence of objective reality recedes. In the shadowy dimension here described (far different from the simple historical fading of "Directive"), mind takes on its own light of glory—what Wordsworth elsewhere calls its "visionary gleam"—just as Wordsworth in "Michael" raises his own EVENING STAR: a sublimation into turnings of verse of the literal one now dimmed and degraded in relative importance.

Against all this, the very particularism of Frost, his tendency in "Directive" and generally to earthward, is the clearer. What I now will urge is how small in him is the capacity for the sublime. He presents a falling, not of starry wonder into landscape, but of word into empty prospects and imagination into tentative fancy, so that there is rarely a *feeling* analogous to the supernatural in his work but only a playing at it.

What, though, of the final directive of "Directive," "Drink and be whole again beyond confusion"? The phrase inevitably summons Frost's famous "Figure a Poem Makes": "It ends in a clarification—not necessarily a great clarification, such as sects and cults are founded on, but a momentary stay against confusion." Yet I have insisted, despite the idealizers, that such clarification is based on disenchanted perception, on desublimation. There is nothing in this figure but figuration, nothing either in "Directive" beyond the moment: indeed, the return to a source in this work may be a return to the capacity of seeing object-as-object, may be a clearing away of complex affective obstacles to gladness, like the children's, at little things.

If Wordsworth asserted that mind and world could interfuse, that their cooperative accomplishment was so mighty as to merit no lower name than creation, Frost in his run-out landscape offers precisely a lowering of poetic claims in general. Little things remain little, for he has neither means nor intention to make great things of small, in the manner of Wordsworth's so-called "higher minds":

> Them the enduring and the transient both
> Serve to exalt; they build up greatest things
> From least suggestions; ever on the watch,
> Willing to work and to be wrought upon,
> They need not extraordinary calls
> To rouse them; in a world of life they live,
> By sensible impressions not enthralled,
> But by their quickening impulse made more prompt
> To hold fit converse with the spiritual world,
> And with the generations of mankind
> Spread over time, past, present, and to come....
> (*Prelude* XIV. 100–110)

Yet we misjudge and undervalue Frost's poetry if we see in it Romantic Dejection. Wordsworth is the greater poet, but he occasionally suffers the defects—bathos, diffuseness, verbal equivocation and intellectual uncertainty—of that greatness. Frost's contraction of scope does more than provide him with capacities for local affection unavailable to Wordsworth: if his modesty also entails its flaws—a witty cuteness, evasiveness, triviality—at its best it does offer clarification, however momentary:

> When in doubt there is always form to go on with. Anyone who has achieved the least form to be sure of it, is lost to the larger excruciations. I think it must stroke faith the right way. The artist, the poet, might be expected to be the most aware of such assurance. But it is really everybody's sanity to live by it. Fortunately, too, no forms are more engrossing than those lesser ones we throw off, like vortex rings of smoke, all our individual enterprise and needing nobody's cooperation; a basket, a letter, a garden, a room, an idea, a picture, a poem. For these we haven't to get a team together to play.

This off-hand listing of "a poem" in such random company would have wounded him who sought "to bind together by passion and knowledge the vast empire of human society" (1800 Preface), but Frost's stance permits him a rhetorical self-assurance that the more ambitious forefather never could attain. In a 1949 lecture fittingly called "Some Obstinacy," Frost stressed that

> The first thing to say is that you've got to start getting up things
> to say to yourself if you want to hold your own. And the pre-
> first thing to say is that you've got to have an own to hold. . . .
>   Don't be afraid of the word. Get up a rigamarole. And I'm
> going to get up and show you some rigamaroles I got up for my
> own defense, you know, for the defense of my position in the
> course of the years.

Frost's corrective to Wordsworth claims that the proper motive behind the
sublimest oratory is self-containment. A poem—rid of its exaltations, its
mists, winds, and gleams—should have a temporary quiddity sufficient to
let us hold our own. The poet's rigamarole will be a form thrust up between
too much and us.

This disenchanted (as it were, "de-mistified") perspective has critical
value for our reading of Wordsworth. It lends some insight, for example,
into the curious induction to "Michael," so full of self-contradiction and
-qualification:

> Beside the brook
> Appears a straggling heap of unhewn stones!
> And to that simple object appertains
> A story—unenriched with strange events,
> Yet not unfit, I deem, for the fireside,
> Or for the summer shade. . . .
>
>   .   .   .   .
>   . . . although it be a history
> Homely and rude, I will relate the same
> And, with yet fonder feeling, for the sake
> Of youthful poets, who among these hills
> Will be my second self when I am gone.
>
> (ll. 16–39)

The "simple object" moves Wordsworth to exclamatory vehemence, which
he automatically undercuts with disclaimer and (in the manner of the Prefaces) litotic turn: the tale is "not unfit." Wordsworth struggles against a
Frostian sense of indifference in the large world, of the poet's small inheritance and small power to pass it on. He directs this "homely and rude"
account to "a *few* natural hearts," to a scattering of successor-poets, yet
even this self-irony must be seen against the grander one, that the induction
which transmits legacy prefaces a tale of *failed* legacy. "Michael," throughout, anticipates a theme of "Directive": a poem affords a momentary stay

against inevitability. Had Wordsworth concerned himself less with the larger excruciations, he might have seen his narrative as rigamarole, as a means of holding his own.

III. A DISTANT STAR

Sadly, Wordsworth may have seen—or sensed—just how much of "Michael" *was* rigamarole. His urge to reset a star (the evening star, significantly, is the classical star of pastoral) is part of his quest for sublimity, and the assertive voice of the induction marks his desire that the poem have, as heavenly bodies are supposed to have, a permanent "influence." Contravening all this is the qualifying, self-effacing voice which emerges whenever a stoical attitude like Frost's toward the matter of legacy or influence intrudes itself. No wonder Frost protested at Cornell that "Michael" went on "too long." Wordsworth's very dilemma forced him into protraction: though he confronted general evidence of the futility of trust in posterity, the entire thrust of his cheerful faith had always been premised on the validity of that trust. Hence his endless animadversions.

Wordsworth's strategy is, as it were, *misguided* rigamarole. Frost knew that feigning must be understood as feigning in order, paradoxically, to have a helpful value; it cannot be rhetorically whipped into value-as-truth. The stay against confusion must be acknowledged as momentary, the figure a poem makes as figuration and not prophetic writ (we should for example "say" our poetry and not feel a need to declaim it).

We can see why Frost should have admired, more straightforwardly than any Wordsworth poem, the "Ode to Duty," the work in which Wordsworth refers to himself as "made lowly wise." The phrase itself, of course, is borrowed from Raphael's advice to Adam in *Paradise Lost* VIII, which comes (aptly) in response to Adam's inquiry about the stars. "Solicit not thy thoughts with matters hid," the archangel urges, and we may like Wordsworth translate the exhortation into an enjoinder against seeking that home in infinitude which, according to *The Prelude*, is the abode of greatness . . . and of sublime poetry. "Ode to Duty," to pun on a modern coinage, shows Wordsworth's abandonment of his quest to be a poetic star.

In describing "Ode to Duty" as "one that I've gotten as much out of in the way of wisdom as any," Frost describes his own derivation of lowly wisdom from a poem which is itself a meditation on derived lowly wisdom, as if a poet's inheritance fell farther and farther from heaven through the generations. Wordsworth seems less diminished by such relentless lapse than Frost, yet his diminutive adaptations of Milton in this ode may signal a reversion to Frostian awareness of the unattainability of super-earthly power and sublime poetic power. Not that Frost is unskeptical enough to identify that power with "the God-head's most benignant grace"; what I emphasize is his common sense of limitation with the Wordsworth of the "Duty" ode, his long-standing acknowledgment that modern efforts to draw lofty influence into the human realm and to pass it on poetically result from solipsistic "confidence misplaced."

"Ode to Duty" looks elsewhere for confidence, traces Wordsworth's submission to a new control: "Me this unchartered freedom tires; / I feel the weight of chance-desires" (ll. 37–38). The very autonomy of the spontaneous, wandering imagination which once lifted from him "the weary weight" of the world is seen itself as a weight, so that the poet now searches for fixity: "My hopes no more must change their name / I long for a repose that ever is the same" (ll. 39–40).

"Ode to Duty" shows, I think, a cleaving to the more modest of the two impulses which constituted the dialectic of "Michael"; it does so even more forthrightly than the "Intimations" ode, also completed in 1804, which nonetheless admits that "nothing can bring back the hour / Of splendour in the grass, of glory in the flower" (ll. 181–82). The old link between starry sublime ("glory") and simple natural object ("flower") is reserved for less ambitious pieces like "I Wandered Lonely As a Cloud" (1804), whose daffodils do appear "continuous as stars." Splendor, glory, and power are no longer figured as perpetual natural immanences in Wordsworth's major turnings of verse. In "Ode to Duty," especially, the poet addresses an abstracted influence: he admits his ripeness to assume "humbler functions" than the effort to connect landscape and sky via imagination.

The poet of the *Recluse* fragment of 1798 had contended that no sublime theme

> ... can breed such fear and awe
> As fall upon us often when we look
> Into our Minds, into the Mind of Man.
> (ll. 791–93)

But in this poem, Duty is the star that falls upon us, the "awful power," the "stern Lawgiver." The renowned Wordsworth is the one attracted to the "silent laws" of the *heart* (see "To My Sister"), or to faith in the mind's capacity to draw astral energy into ordinary objects. Frost's Wordsworth resuscitates a severely hierarchical cosmology:

> Flowers laugh before thee on their beds
> And fragrance in thy footing treads;
> Thou dost preserve the stars from wrong;
> And the most ancient heavens, through thee,
>   are fresh and strong.

Degrees of power and influence are strictly apportioned and "chartered" here: man is, so to say, higher than the flowers and lower than the stars, each of which in turn occupies a separate realm from the other. Indeed, the visible stars are inferior ones (preserved by Duty): above them are invisible heavens; then Duty, who herself is thrice removed from ultimate power: "Daughter of the voice of God!" The universe shades off into pure inscrutability beyond its perceptible margin. The poet addresses Duty because she is all of heavenly influence that he can intuit; she is his figure, his translation into moral imperative, of hidden might. And she is presented as a superior star (she is "a light to guide," "the light of truth," having the capacity to lead us on "a blissful course") merely because such figuration, deeply contingent on our limited vision, is as close as the "language really used by men" can reach toward genuine sublimity. A star, withdrawn from us, and relatively constant to us, is simply a model for integrity. "I think," says Frost, "that's where I'd like to say two or three lines out of that . . . , as if they were embossed on the page. As if they were embossed. For instance: 'And happy will our nature be / When love is an unerring light.' "

Frost, however elliptically, approves Wordsworth's message concerning the fixity and remoteness of the source of influence: and he can himself point to benefits in our attendant assumption of lowliness, urging us exactly to "Take Something Like a Star," which,

> *Not even stooping from its sphere,*
> . . . asks a little of us here.
> It asks of us a certain height,
> So when at times the mob is swayed
> To carry praise or blame too far,
> We may take something like a star
> To stay our minds on and be staid.
>   (emphasis added)

If unerring light prompts no sublime flight, merely asking "a little of us," the height which we do reach in our modesty is at least a "certain height." Frost's star-poem (companion piece to "Closed for Good" in the Afterword of *Collected Poems*, 1949) seeks security in a world which historically and ontologically works toward our diminishment; and there is evidence that Wordsworth, like Frost—movingly conscious of how difficult it is to receive and transmit poetic legacy—took late comfort in such purged aspiration.

DAVID BROMWICH

Wordsworth, Frost, Stevens
and the Poetic Vocation

The following notes on two modern poems were prompted by some reservations about the recent criticism of Wordsworth. That criticism agrees on the importance of "the image," and shows in detail how the image is fitted to the particular occasions of "the crisis poem." I want to acknowledge these ideas at the outset because I too will be relying on them. But the image has come to stand for two different things: first, a picture which has enduring worth for the poet because it is a fact; and second, an imagining that began as such a picture, has been revolved in the mind, and is prized as a thing of the mind. These two sorts of image are related through the change in meaning by which the first brought forth the second, and we now read Wordsworth with the second ascendant, the first being understood as a distant part of its genealogy. My reservation is that the fact-image had a moral significance for Wordsworth which the mind-image alone can never have. It signalled a connection between the poet and other men; and this was true, no matter what the poet's relation to the object that yielded the image, whether he disturbed its perfect repose, or sent it wandering, or found himself strangely invigorated beside it; whereas for us, the connection has become less and less interesting. We are concerned instead with what the image helps the poet to do for himself.

This was perhaps inevitable in an age dominated by Yeats, with his thoroughly inward sense of vocation. For us the image has been purged of fact and the crisis poem released from its connection with other men. But

From *Studies in Romanticism* 21, no. 1 (Spring 1982). © 1982 by the Trustees of Boston University.

Wordsworth himself wished for no such release. He tried to think of poetry in conjunction with other human pursuits, and of the poet as both minister and witness to the needs of others. His eventual failure to meet the conditions of his double office, "by words, / Which speak of nothing more than what we are"—a failure by degrees, of which he left evidence of his own recognition by degrees—produced the poems which at once lament the withdrawal this implies within his vocation, and celebrate the survival of his gift in some form. Wordsworth regarded such poems as a personal response to a personal disappointment. They nevertheless became a pattern to his successors, and one reason why they should have done so is obvious. Wordsworth was the first lyric allegorist of the poetic career. He set the terms in which the whole subject of vocation presents itself to any modern poet. Yet the modern poet as a rule has conceived no Wordsworthian ambitions for the humanizing influence of poetry, and without these nothing compels him to repeat Wordsworth's lament. Looking back at "Tintern Abbey," "Resolution and Independence," the "Ode to Duty" and "Immortality" ode, and "Elegiac Stanzas" on Peele Castle, he may feel a good deal less reluctant than Wordsworth to assert that the poet's sympathy with others is really a bondage.

While alluding to Wordsworth, his successors have thus been able to treat solely as a poetic gain what he described in some measure as a human loss. It will be plain by now that the poem I have most in view is "Resolution and Independence." From its plot the later poet has usually had to abstract a few bold features: what is left out, except in attenuated hints, is the poet's continuing relation to something other than his own mastery. Here, modern commentators on Wordsworth have been guided by modern poetry, in a way that is seldom acknowledged. For those who discuss the poetic crisis solely in poetic terms are interpreting Wordsworth in line with what his successors have made of him. On literary-historical grounds one may want to retard this process; it makes Wordsworth's period too neatly continuous with ours. But I believe that more than literary history is at stake. The modern understanding of Wordsworth has fostered great poems, and much thoughtful criticism, but the damage has been great also. What I have to say about two specimens of the Wordsworth tradition is mainly intended to recall the undertone of regret with which an early critic and successor first pronounced him the poet of the egotistical sublime.

Frost's "Two Tramps in Mud Time" and Stevens's "The Course of a Particular" show these poets about as remote from each other as they ever get, in the entire range of their practice, and between the poems themselves no affinity will be claimed, other than their shared descent from "Resolution and Independence." Let me begin by rehearsing in the simplest terms the Wordsworthian situation that all three poems ask us to contemplate. In an unpromising landscape, lit by a change of weather from stormy to fair—a happy change, which nevertheless reminds us of the vicissitudes of all outer and inner weather—a poet filled with unsettling thoughts about his vocation is suddenly brought face to face with a common laborer, or one who suffers the common fate of men and not the uncommon fate of poets. Already I must qualify this, because the poems make the scene visible in different degrees, and the second figure is less clearly realized as we move from Wordsworth to Frost to Stevens. At every step of the way he becomes more strictly a creature of figuration. Indeed, Frost puts his tramps into the title partly to call attention to their absence from the poem, while Stevens reduces the figure to a thing heard but never seen, and that in a negative clause: the "human cry" is one of the things that the cry of leaves is not.

But to return to the meeting of poet and laborer: the important distinction between them seems to be that the laborer has an immediate result to show for his work—a pile of so much wood, a gathering of so many leeches—whereas the poet has none. The poet may be haunted by what he knows of the waste of powers, his own and that of his brother poets, yet he has a place of work to call his own. The laborer, on the other hand, is at home in no place; he may live in constant fear of adversity, yet somehow his spirit remains untroubled. The special nature of the poet's labor apparently needs to be explained, and even justified: this is what the Poem of Resolution and Independence must do, touched all the while by a suspicion that the making of more poems will depend on its success.

Since the link with "Resolution and Independence" will be clear to many readers of "The Course of a Particular," I will give more sustained attention to "Two Tramps in Mud Time." It may help at first to think of Frost's poem as a kind of riddle. At some level he knew all along that he was occupied with another version of Wordsworth's poem, but part of his "fooling" with the reader was to withhold his definitive clue until the middle of the poem, when many other pieces had fallen into place. It comes in the fourth stanza, with the unexpected appearance of a bluebird:

> A bluebird comes tenderly up to alight
> And turns to the wind to unruffle a plume,
> His song so pitched as not to excite
> A single flower as yet to bloom.

To the question, Why this, in a poem about tramps?—the answer is that the bird, along with the topic it introduces, is entirely within its rights by authority of the jay, the magpie, the hare, and the "plashy earth" of the misted sunny moor that occupy the opening stanzas of "Resolution and Independence." It is of the essence of both poems that they should work hard to separate landscape from the scene of labor proper: the pleasures of landscape will belong to the poet alone, and be felt at the intervals of his self-questioning; to the figure who confronts the poet, on the other hand, landscape hardly exists; it thus works its way through the poem as a double counterpoint, always present, but vividly present only to the poet, and much of the time not even to him.

Looking back, one discovers an earlier touch of craft relevant to the allusion. This is the modified alexandrine—a pentameter line to vary a tetrameter base, at the end of the third stanza—which has the look and feel of the Spenserian stanza one associates with "Resolution and Independence":

> The sun was warm but the wind was chill.
> You know how it is with an April day
> When the sun is out and the wind is still,
> You're one month on in the middle of May.
> But if you so much as dare to speak,
> A cloud comes over the sunlit arch,
> A wind comes off a frozen peak,
> And you're two months back in the middle of March.
>
> (ll. 17–24)

The last line, it could be argued, is really a crowded tetrameter, but against all objections I would maintain that it is still an alexandrine to the eye, and so far part of the "in and outdoor schooling" Frost's readers are advised to have.

Two further clues are at once subtler and more persuasive. First, the Wordsworthian sentiment of Frost's confession—"That day, giving a loose to my soul, / I spent on the unimportant wood"—with which one connects such moments as the "sweet mood" mentioned in "Nutting," when "The heart luxuriates with indifferent things, / Wasting its kindliness on stocks and stones." And then, the emergence of a second figure from a ground of undifferentiated matter, as from a sedimentary deposit: Frost's two strangers coming "Out of the mud" bring to mind that other stranger whom we first glimpse "As a huge stone is sometimes seen to lie / Couched on the bald top of an eminence," and later, "Like a sea-beast crawled forth."

With these parallels established, one is surprised at a difference that remains. Frost gets through his poem effortlessly, and *without* the tramps.

He can do so because in this version of Wordsworth's poem, Frost himself is poet and laborer at once. Imagine now a somewhat modified plot for "Resolution and Independence." Wordsworth looks at the shifting weather, thinks to himself—What a splendid day for a walk!—takes up his staff and sallies out on a leech-gathering expedition, feeling solid as a rock. On his way he meets an old man, the oldest he ever saw, whose life seems to have been lived on the boundaries of misery, and who offers to do the leech-gathering for him. "He wants my job for pay," Wordsworth mutters, and though he admits that this man's claim to the work outweighs his own, he keeps on with it anyway, exhilarated by thoughts of the different virtues of his two adopted vocations, and how they grow richer by being united. This, with the necessary changes, is Frost's story:

> Nothing on either side was said.
> They knew they had but to stay their stay
> And all their logic would fill my head:
> As that I had no right to play
> With what was another man's work for gain.
> My right might be love but theirs was need.
> And where the two exist in twain
> Theirs was the better right—agreed.
>
> But yield who will to their separation,
> My object in living is to unite
> My avocation and my vocation
> As my two eyes make one in sight.
> (ll. 57–68)

What a peculiar and original story it is, once we hear "Resolution and Independence" as part of the context Frost evokes. Notice, above all, how completely the sentiment has been altered in the parting gesture, from a widening of sympathy brought on by the recognition of human endurance, to what looks like a rejection of sympathy and charity alike. And yet this cannot be the whole story, if only because we cannot make it tally with the swell and uplift of Frost's concluding lines. Frost has an early poem, also about an experience of charity denied, a poem very roughly parallel to "Two Tramps in Mud Time," called "Love and a Question." There a bridegroom on his wedding night finds a stranger at the door, and though willing to give him a dole of bread and a purse, refuses him shelter for the night: the desire aglow in the "bridal house" is too precious for sharing. In that poem too we have the dismissal of the wanderer, and the moralized closing stanza by Frost, but in a situation more congenial to his point of view. "Love and a Question" is a charming poem. "Two Tramps in Mud Time" is not, nor does it mean to be. Its effect is to limit and qualify the humanizing effect of Wordsworth's poem, and in doing so it involves Frost in a curious drama of self-exposure, of a kind that few poets of his cunning would have wished to trace beyond the first hesitant steps.

Still, one may be mystified by the high spirits Frost discovers at the end, and by the triumphal cadence that goes with them:

> Only where love and need are one,
> And the work is play for mortal stakes,
> Is the deed ever really done
> For Heaven and the future's sakes.
>
> (ll.69–72)

I think Frost got this tone from Arnold, who was always among his favorite poets. One poem of Arnold's, "Palladium," he seems to have returned to again and again: the soul to the body is as the Palladium, "high 'mid rock and wood," to the soldiers fighting on the battlefield below; so long as it stands, Troy cannot fall; and, with the soul and body it cannot be wholly otherwise. Frost had this in his ear when he wrote "Trial by Existence," for *A Boy's Will*, and it was with him again for "Two Tramps in Mud Time." I quote the final stanzas of "Palladium" in which Arnold imagines the earthly battles renewed:

> Then we shall rust in shade, or shine in strife,
> And fluctuate 'twixt blind hopes and blind despairs,
> And fancy that we put forth all our life,
> And never know how with the soul it fares.
>
> Still doth the soul, from its lone fastness high,
> Upon our life a ruling effluence send;
> And when it fails, fight as we will, we die,
> And while it lasts, we cannot wholly end.

This need not have appealed to Frost strictly for the poetry, for there was something else, in the cultural predicament of both men, which made him recognize Arnold as a natural ally. Arnold, to himself, was a spirit wandering between two worlds, between, among other things, the world of romanticism, which he conscientiously but never very cheerfully cast into the outer darkness, and the world of utilitarianism, which he could never love or accept. The result for his poetry was that sense of being embattled but deprived of an aim which makes even the end of "Palladium" sound oddly unhappy, for so happy a conceit. Frost, it seems to me, was attracted to the *soldiering* rhetoric because, though from different historical causes, he had the same sense of being embattled without having an enemy properly in sight. The dimensions of the conflict may be suggested by two facts: that Frost was a product of nineteenth-century New England, and that "Two Tramps in Mud Time" is a poem of the New Deal. In the thirties, Richard Poirier writes,

> Frost began to suspect that the metaphors, including that of *laissez-faire*, which governed his thinking and his poetry were being substantially displaced within the national consciousness by two others. On the one hand, there were metaphors of "waste-land," or apocalyptic disillusion, against which individual re-sistance was presumably useless; and on the other, the metaphor of "planning," of the New Deal, of provision, which, as Frost saw it, was designed to relieve the individual of responsibility for his own fate.
>
> That was the essential problem, and measured against it Frost's lapses of taste, his occasional paranoiac inaccuracies, and his petty complaints should be treated as inessential.

Without treating "Two Tramps in Mud Time" as a lapse of taste one may regard it as a striking instance of his predicament. He has to be both poet and laborer to make the point about his independence; he has to begin with Wordsworth's argument, because Wordsworth's is the great poem in English about the poetic consciousness and its sustaining need of sympathy; the comparison with Wordsworth makes Frost seem colder, as all refusal seems colder than indifference; but he will deal with it how he can, for he is determined to write the poem. Poetry and sympathy are just the matters about which Frost wants to tell us something shocking. "My vocation *and* avocation: let others find theirs if they can; the best help I can give is to tell them so."

Certainly the allusion is a remarkable piece of daring, and could only have been risked by a great poet at the height of his self-confidence. It is that; and yet, in almost any reader's first response to the poem, one impres-sion remains fixed: that Frost has not finally earned his eloquence, that his triumph is a little hollow. The impression remains I think because we have never been shown the distance between Frost's vocation and his avocation, and hence between his nature and that of the tramps. When we see Words-worth and the leech-gatherer together, we learn to our amazement what different beings they are. Frost too wants to make us feel this, so long as we say afterwards, "But he contains the two tramps; they don't contain him." But we do not say this, because the whole poem has been tipped off balance by a touch of bad faith. At the bottom of it, Poirier believes, is a distrust of poetry. I agree but would add: a distrust of being seen to be a poet. The poem lets us see the two tramps, and a man who we know is a poet because he writes poems, this one among them. But Frost-as-poet is not, so to speak, figured into the poem. To have done so would have been to take on the privilege but also the vulnerability of the poet's situation, and the ambivalence that they imply when taken together. It would not have meant going over to Wordsworth's side on the question of sympathy, even if we could be sure just what that means in a poem like "Resolution and Independence." But the stark improbables of the scene with its two figures, the strange out-feeling that passes from poet to laborer, and the "help and stay secure," or stay against confusion which the poet gets in return: these were the things Frost had to confront. His poem had to be much longer than it is, simply to accommodate the full view of the question to which he pledged himself by alluding to Wordsworth. But he escapes by a trick of foreshortening, in the last stanza, of which the tenor is self-sacrifice, and the vehicle sacrifice of others.

By a full view I mean the dialectic to which we feel Wordsworth has committed himself when he writes:

> My whole life I have lived in pleasant thought,
> As if life's business were a summer mood;
> As if all needful things would come unsought
> To genial faith, still rich in genial good;
> But how can He expect that others should
> Build for him, sow for him, and at his call
> Love him, who for himself will take no heed at all.

There Wordsworth steps out of a race humming with labor and vocation, as a special self. After that there was no turning back. Frost, perhaps from an outsize respect for the rhetorical leverage afforded by the style of the ordinary man, never does step forward. Yet he is writing a kind of poem in which this reticence must be fatal. The poet and laborer may indeed be the same person: but we need to see the poet. Frost's reluctance to come to grips with both vocations—a reluctance that really makes us wonder, which is his vocation? which his avocation?—left its stamp on the rousing last stanza. It is a fine enough sort of eloquence that Frost treats us to, a sort that, like Arnold's, can come of an evasion, and cheer us for a while.

But it is not quite in earnest. "Two Tramps in Mud Time," could he have gone the whole length and realized the poem that he projected in the shape of an allusion, would have justified Frost's own metaphors of self-reliance more directly than anything else he wrote.

In contrast "The Course of a Particular" may seem to require no supplement at all to assist our understanding. None, at any rate, beyond the assurance that when Stevens writes, "And being part is an exertion that declines," he is making a distant reply to Whitman, whom he had once pictured as the prophet of poetry and life, with his beard of fire, his staff a leaping flame, "singing and chanting the things that are part of him" ("Like Decorations in a Nigger Cemetery," ll. 1–6). Besides, so far as the poem refers us to any earlier utterance, it may seem enough to recall "The Snow Man" and "the misery in the sound of the wind, / In the sound of a few leaves," the words that mark the opening chapter of Stevens's lifelong effort to subdue the "Ode to the West Wind" to the beauty of innuendoes. The snow man must have been cold a long time not to be moved by the pathos of this particular. In "The Course of a Particular" on the contrary, one "holds off and merely hears the sound": the poet *is* cold, and no longer part of everything; and the exertion once implied by hearing the human appeal in the sound, has now declined. One has grown at last severe enough to be unconcerned, to live "in the absence of fantasia."

The poem's immense dignity and power have much to do with the weight it carries in every feature, the deliberation with which it declares by every step of its forward motion that it is the work of a very old man. In what it asserts, however, this poem is as shocking as "Two Tramps in Mud Time," and as firmly antithetical to the "distress" of the Wordsworthian encounter. So I can offer one strong reason for considering "The Course of a Particular" with Wordsworth instead of Shelley in the background. It is, that while Stevens's largest piece of furniture is evidently Shelley's fiction of the leaves, his motive seems to me Wordsworthian. Again, such constituents as will serve have been abstracted from "Resolution and Independence." The poet, as poet, is brought face to face with life, as life, which— like the man half-rock, half-man, on the lonely moor—goes on without him, in a way that is chastening to regard. Stevens tells us that he can no longer be moved by the particular that has been his, the cry; but still, *that it merely is* appears to be a necessary condition for his poetry; it is the sign of a larger endurance that implies endurance for himself.

As an interpretation of Wordsworth "The Course of a Particular" is reductive but far from absurd. We know that Wordsworth, in composing "Resolution and Independence," originally wrote a substantial monologue for the leech-gatherer; in revising, his aim was to reduce this second human figure to the last bareness of mere being; and he told Sara Hutchinson, who could not see the point of the poem, that his concern had never been with anything about the man but, as it were, simply *that* the man: "What is brought forward? 'A lonely place, a Pond,' 'by which an old man *was*, far from all house and home': not stood, not sat, but *was*." Stevens's poem contains a line that corresponds perfectly to the reading of Wordsworth sanctioned here by Wordsworth himself: "One feels the life of that which gives life as it is." The title, "The Course of a Particular," I take to mean that the sense of one's own engagement with being has run its course throughout one's life: memories of a thing, and the present consciousness of it, have become a spot of time purged of all inessentials; until at last the thing stands "in the most naked simplicity possible," to adapt another phrase of Wordsworth's from the same letter to Sara Hutchinson. The sound concerns no one at all, and yet it still is, and poetry still gets written. Stevens, it is true, had looked forward to this sense of the life of poetry as early as "The Snow Man." But that was a very programmatic poem, and reads comparatively like a manifesto. By the time he wrote, "One feels the life of that which gives life as it is," Stevens knew that he had grown cold enough, without ever ceasing to think of the particular and its wanderings. His composure had become a full fact.

But does not Stevens in his own way suppress one element of his work as a revisionist? The suppression is of course less imposing than Frost's, it has no broad consequences for the shape of the poem, we are made to feel throughout that Stevens has spent a long time working at poetry. Nevertheless there is something—a deflection, a refinement—which by softening the harsher contrasts of the Wordsworth plot, prevents us from seeing clearly what Stevens has done with it, and so works out as irony. I am thinking of the phrase, "One holds off and merely hears the cry." Now, in common speech, one usually holds off from something one will come back to: "Let me hold off on this"; "No, I want to hold off on the parties until I get to know that crowd better." But Stevens does not have it in mind ever to come back to the cry, except as it echoes in the ear. Once gone, it is gone forever. This is in fact an extreme instance of litotes, close in spirit to the withheld denouements which had been proved on the pulses of Stevens's generation by its leading writer of prose: "Well, you better not think about it." Its value for the poem is to make us worry less scrupulously about the closure of all relations effected by Stevens's detachment. We cease to be troubled by it, for it seems in this light a familiar and honorable sort of patience, born of its share of sympathy and of suffering. The poem can imply all this while saying only, with complete honesty, "I have heard the cry; it ran its course; I need it no more." The understatement thus becomes an apology because we are meant to reflect on Stevens's career, and to remember how often, long after "The Snow Man," he had charted the particular's bearings: in "Sad Strains of a Gay Waltz," and "Mozart, 1935" ("The snow is falling / And the streets are full of cries"); in "Like Decorations in a Nigger Cemetery," the coda to Notes toward a Supreme Fiction, and "Esthétique du Mal" ("Pain is human.... This is a part of the sublime / From which we shrink"). My impression is that the earlier poems or passages are far steadier in tone than the later ones. Stevens would have had reasons of craft as well as temperament for telling us in an ambiguous phrase that his holding-off would be extended indefinitely.

Some differences of concern that separate Frost and Stevens in much of their work ought to emerge from comparing the stances they adopt to "Resolution and Independence." What both try is to internalize the Wordsworthian encounter with the second figure. Frost all but eliminates the figure in favor of the poet, and at the same time he eliminates the pathos of the poetic vocation itself. This last is the only thing Stevens finds interesting, but he has the advantage that it is the only thing he pretends to find interesting. "Resolution and Independence" addresses itself to the continuity of poetry for the poet, and the justification of poetry to the world. Of those concerns Stevens has to do mainly with the first, the question of continuity, and Frost mainly with the second, the question of justification: the division is writ large throughout their careers. And yet, Wordsworth's comprehensiveness in this respect goes a very small way toward explaining the stature of "Resolution and Independence." He schools our admiration for the poem not only by his movement from one concern to the other, but equally by the way he discloses himself in the process of movement:

> The old Man still stood talking by my side;
> But now his voice to me was like a stream
> Scarce heard; nor word from word could I divide;
> And the whole body of the Man did seem
> Like one whom I had met with in a dream;
> Or like a man from some far region sent,
> To give me human strength, by apt admonishment.
>
> (ll. 106–12)

The poem moves from justification to continuity, and Wordsworth displaces the leech-gatherer's admonishment with his own "killing thoughts." The familiarity of the stream-as-eloquence topic makes the work of the transition almost inaudible. Yet Wordsworth marks for us each distinct moment of the fade-out and usurpation. In the first line the leech-gatherer is wholly present; in the second he is absorbed into the metonymy of voice; from this follows the metaphor of the stream; and finally the vision. It is here that the comparison with Frost and Stevens becomes most telling. For Frost allows his tramps to lapse from the poem unaccountably. And Stevens begins "The Course of a Particular" at a point near the end of the fade-out: what he hears is only the voice, unembodied; and to judge by this poem, one would say that in the past it had concerned him only as *materia poetica*.

Yet elsewhere in his poetry Stevens allows for a more generous response. In *Notes toward a Supreme Fiction*, for example, he uses "image" in a sense entirely consistent with Wordsworth's decision to retain the leech-gatherer as a distinct presence: "the difficultest rigor is forthwith, / On the image of what we see, to catch from that / Irrational moment its unreasoning." About the sort of figure that this effort preserves he says, "These are not things transformed./ Yet we are shaken by them as if they were." So too has the leech-gatherer remained untransformed, to repeat his answer when Wordsworth renews his question. Repetition is here the brute circumstance that discloses all the intractability of being. The leech-gatherer is *there*. Only later, as an after-image, when Wordsworth imagines him in his mind's eye still wandering about the lonely moor, does he begin to be transformed by the mind. But this final movement of Wordsworth's imagination gives no more promise of a self-sufficient triumph than does the hope he confides to Dorothy at the end of "Tintern Abbey," that he may read his former pleasures in the shooting lights of her eyes. It is an uneasy compensation, and he risks turning the leech-gatherer, like Dorothy, into a machine that can be dismissed once it has served its purpose. Since he knows the risk, "there is a struggle, there is a resistance involved," a scruple about his actual relation to the leech-gatherer, and about the cost of making him only a thing of the mind's eye. He neither has nor cares to have the pride that Frost and Stevens exhibit in overcoming that resistance.

Now and then in these pages I have used the word "sympathy," always with some hesitation. I am aware how far the criticism of Wordsworth in our time has been associated with a rejection of Arnoldian ideas about him, and with this rejection I agree wholeheartedly. Wordsworth does not seem to me the poet "Of joy in widest commonalty spread." Nor do I believe that it was a joy of communion which passed between Wordsworth and the leech-gatherer, in either direction. Sympathy may therefore be a misleading word for what I mean; "acknowledgment" or "recognition" might be better. But I have stayed with it because its very etymology includes what is central to my argument: a feeling that touches some second figure, and that could not come into being without it. Granted Wordsworth puts such figures to a use which even a liberalism more modest than Arnold's can never endorse. A comment like A. D. Nuttall's on "The Old Cumberland Beggar" suggests in addition that the poems in which he does so are more closely related to "Resolution and Independence" than one cares to remember:

> There is a moralising argument and I had better confess at once that I find it repellent. It turns on an inversion of the normal order of ethical discourse. Instead of saying that charity is good because it relieves distress, Wordsworth is virtually saying that distress is good because it provides stimulus and scope for charity. Thus a sort of meta-ethical realm is introduced. It is important that men should be happy, but it is far more important that charity should *exist*.

But this takes less from the humanity of the poem than it may seem to do. Wordsworth, even on this view, still keeps the beggar wandering, in the belief that he may some day encounter him again. A search of all Stevens's poetry will produce no such figure. One may, on the other hand, find something resembling him in Frost, but never in a poem where the poet also appears as himself. The great difference between Wordsworth and his modern successors, I have begun to think, lies not so much in "the love of man" as in his simple copresence with another figure, radically unassimilable to himself, and the troubling possibilities that this brings. The egotistical sublime could reach its height when it existed in tension with such possibilities.

HERBERT MARKS

The Counter-Intelligence
of Robert Frost

I. WHY THE STARS TWINKLE

When Robert Frost presents himself to the reader in the late poem "Directive" as one "who only has at heart your getting lost," or has the Keeper in *A Masque of Mercy* declare to his fugitive alter ego, "Some people want you not to understand them, / But I want you to understand me wrong," he is playing on the interaction of revelation and concealment—a theological commonplace, consecrated for English literature in Touchstone's demonstration that "the truest poetry is the most faining...." The problem of feigning figures prominently in all Frost's work, as a stylistic tendency toward the gnomic, but also as a theme. Consider a less obvious clue, the preface he wrote in 1924 to the little-known *Memoirs of the Notorious Stephen Burroughs*, in which he praises the Massachusetts imposter for his "sophisticated wickedness, the kind that knows its grounds and can twinkle." Burroughs had a flair for irony, and Frost, musing toward the end of the essay on his conversion to Catholicism, appears to have recognized their shared affinities:

> I should like to have heard his reasons for winding up in the Catholic Church. I can conceive of their being honest. Probably he was tired of his uncharted freedom out of jail and wanted to be moral and a Puritan again as when a child, but this time under a cover where he couldn't be made fun of by the intellectuals. The course might commend itself to the modern Puritan (what there is left of the modern Puritan).

From *The Yale Review* 71, no. 4 (July 1982). © 1982 by Yale University.

Though couched humorously, two serious notions are here advanced in defense of Burrough's "hypocrisy." One is the necessity of concealment, the other is the flaccidity of unconstrained freedom, and, taken together, they are among the central articles of Frost's own personal and poetic creed.

The canny style of engagement is characteristic of Frost, who like Bel's favorite poet in *A Masque of Mercy* seems to have espoused a "doctrine of the Seven Poses." "We like to talk in parables and in hints and in indirections," he explained to an audience at Amherst College, "whether from diffidence or some other instinct." Perhaps the instinct is self-preservation, or less starkly, the desire to rival God, whose glory it is to conceal things, according to the biblical proverb. Its counterpart, in any case, is the instinct to seek things out, called by the same proverb the glory of kings; and it is disheartening to observe that in our less regal moods we tend to relegate each other's evasions to the realm of confessional hide-and-seek—as when Lawrance Thompson, in his introduction to Frost's letters, presumes to excuse the poet's "masks" by reminding us of his "excruciating sensitivities." Three critical dicta are accordingly in order: that masking is not necessarily a personal symptom; that poetry can exist only as veiled or elusive meaning—Frost has called it metaphor; and that these two precepts imply one another. Admittedly, Frost often provokes some reductive psychologizing even as he reprehends it: one thinks of his admonition to Sidney Cox, "I have written to keep the over curious out of the secret places of my mind." But the invitation, "You come too," at the front of the collected poems is of another, more generous order, and we misprize it badly if we suppose that poetic masks are something behind which it is our privilege or duty to peer. As Frost pointedly remarked in a letter to Thompson, "The right virtue of a natural reader is the nice ability to tell always when a poem is being figurative. . . . A little of the low-down on motivation goes a long way."

This is not to deny that personal anxieties, including a fear of exposure, contributed to the shaping of Frost's personae. Yet his reasons for resisting biographical criticism go beyond the desire for privacy, and informers whetted by such seemingly transparent poses as the folksy philosopher or the good grey poet would do well to pause before exposing themselves. For Frost, any effort to go behind the masks is finally not only slavish but futile; for the "true person" is an endlessly receding ideal, valuable as a stimulus or lure, but proof against definition. A similar premise underlies Frost's resolve to "spoil" his correspondence with Cox "by throwing it into confusion the way God threw the speech of the builders of the tower of Babel into confusion." What sounds like arrogant mystagogy is at bottom a shrewd reminder that the confusion of tongues and the fall of the tower were manifestations of an already extant condition: that given the state of Noah's descendants, our projects for arriving anywhere directly must collapse of their own accord. The cadres at Babel failed to reach heaven by reason of the same law that preserves or isolates the author from his readers, or the friend from his familiars; and these varied restrictions are finally inseparable. When Frost's Jonah confesses, "I think I may have got God wrong entirely," the Keeper only echoes in reply, "All of us get each other pretty wrong."

If the face-to-face vision of God and the poet relieved of his personae are interchangeable fictions, it is their mythical complement, the naked or public muse, who flits through "Paul's Wife," a poem that explores the necessity of concealment from multiple vantage points. Frost's strategy in the poem is clever. His yarning narrator, after posing the problem of Paul's refusal to be questioned about his rumored marriage, first relates a series of anonymous explanations, for the most part based on the self-defeating view that Paul really has no wife, or that "the obscurity's a fraud to cover nothing," to quote Job's words from *A Masque of Reason*. Ideally, such reductiveness should serve as a warning, but the more generous observations of the backwoods magister Murphy elicit a second variety of interpretive shortcuts, this time from the reader.

The story he tells is that Paul took a log the mill had rejected, carved out the pith and carried it to the pond, where it dissolved and reemerged a girl. Recognition followed, and the couple set off for a niche in the mountains, pursued at a distance by Murphy and his gang of spying loggers. There the new bride shone like a star, till shouts of tribute and a flying bottle broke the charm, and the girl vanished. As usual with Frost, the apparently simple report abounds with symbols and mythical echoes. The contrasts between the mill and the jackknife, the empty bottle and the transfiguring pond, trade on familiar Frostian emblems; while the generation of Paul's native Anadyomene from the pithy log corresponds nicely to the birth of Venus in Hesiod. But the serious difficulty, and with it the real interest of the poem, only begins with the conclusion, in which Murphy finally offers his own interpretation of Paul's evasiveness:

> Paul put on all those airs
> About his wife to keep her to himself.

> Paul was what's called a terrible possessor.
> Owning a wife with him meant owning her.
> She wasn't anybody else's business,
> Either to praise her or so much as name her,
> And he'd thank people not to think of her.
> Murphy's idea was that a man like Paul
> Wouldn't be spoken to about a wife
> In any way the world knew how to speak.

At first, these lines seem to echo the arguments from self-preservation and delicacy of feeling suggested by Thompson. Accordingly, they compel two trains of thought: one psychological, about the makeup of the "man like Paul" so leery of intrusion; the second political, about the makeup of the world to which his elusiveness is the fit response. Such readings, like the arguments they would have Murphy echoing, are not so much invalid as incomplete. They allow us to suppose that, given a tougher hide, or a world somehow smarter or better mannered, Paul would have been glad to haul his wife back to camp and, like Len the husband in "A Servant to Servants," compel her to cook for the boys. They neglect, in other words, that necessary correspondence between masking and metaphor—the idea that since language is by nature metaphorical, it must inevitably conceal or misrepresent whatever it tries to convey. Ultimately, for Frost, "*any* way the world knew how to speak" to Paul about his wife must have sounded like slander.

I have been suggesting that a basic theme of Frost's work is the paradoxical alliance of truth and concealment. Another, as I shall try to show, speaks to the mutual dependence of freedom and restraint. In a sense, these two antitheses really express a single paradox, the first in epistemological, the second in physical (or ethical) terms. But I prefer to acknowledge the difference between them, and so the power necessary to yoke them together; for it is precisely here, in the fact that Frost's vision spanned both poles, embracing the physical and the mental and making them cohere, that his accomplishment is most impressive.

Perhaps the finest product of this coherence is "The Silken Tent," a poem that conveys both the interdependence of freedom and restraint and, when read allusively, the higher economics of feigning:

> She is as in a field a silken tent
> At midday when a sunny summer breeze
> Has dried the dew and all its ropes relent,
> So that in guys it gently sways at ease,

And its supporting central cedar pole,
That is its pinnacle to heavenward
And signifies the sureness of the soul,
Seems to owe naught to any single cord,
But strictly held by none, is loosely bound
By countless silken ties of love and thought
To everything on earth the compass round,
And only by one's going slightly taut
In the capriciousness of summer air
Is of the slightest bondage made aware.

The tent is a figure for poetic incarnation, and the fourteen lines of the poem, which uses the restrictions and compartmentalizations of the Shakespearean sonnet to achieve its single sentence, seem themselves a formal embodiment of the meaning they convey. This correspondence of form to content is reflected in the smallest details: the description of the central pole, for example, which is placed in the central quatrain; or the final couplet, which illustrates its own slight "bondage" to formal restraints by "going taut" as preannounced. On a larger scale, the whole sonnet unfolds within the bounds set by the initial simile, in illustration of the inevitable impingement, restrictive yet sustaining, of metaphor on direct expression. As the momentum of the sentence develops, we are tempted to forget such a flexible parenthesis, just as we tend for the most part to ignore the frames within which our thoughts and feelings run their course. Twice therefore Frost brings us back to the ground of reality by calling attention to the metaphorical relation with deliberate gestures which are themselves "silken ties." In line 7, the central pole is surprised at its work of fictional identification and exposed for what it really is, an index that "signifies." The second time, in line 10, the relation no longer needs to be enforced. So close is the control that it is allowed to dissolve—the fusion the poem sets out to interdict taking place, by leave, at the very moment its ban resounds most clearly. It is a wonderful moment, the love and thought which are the soul's rarest ornaments merging with the ties that keep the tent erect in a necessarily contingent freedom. The balanced tensions, appropriately, are both erotic and metaphysical. The gracefulness enveloping the figure binds with its earthward pull the virile thrust toward the sublime, so that the complete structure remains at once open toward, yet apt to withstand, the animating breeze as it presides over the conclusion.

Not the least of Frost's triumphs here is his transvaluation of "the earthly tent," a prominent image in ascetic literature used by Paul in his

Second Letter to the Corinthians to figure the temporary abode of the soul. For Paul, the tent suggests the eventuality of being "swallowed up" into a "heavenly dwelling"; in the sonnet, all hint of the provisional is banished. To be sure, Frost preserves the Pauline delight in paradox, but he fosters it for its own sake, unabashedly, rather than in the name of what transcends or resolves it. Where one senses cautious denigration behind Paul's testimony that "we have this treasure in earthen vessels," in Frost's revision, physical embodiment becomes an occasion for pure celebration: not the "earthly" but the "silken" tent.

Especially in Frost's earlier work, the power of such biblical echoes comes from their compression—the layers of connotation through which they are forced to pass. Symbolic locus of the illimitable Shekinah in the Pentateuch, figure in John for the indwelling of the Logos, associated with poetic incarnation in *Paradise Regained* and Emerson's "Terminus," the tent is a potentially cumbersome legacy which Frost, by his very reticence, manages to appropriate. In the late poem "Kitty Hawk," by contrast, the economic parallel between poetics and Christology comes to the surface in lines that stand as a sort of creedal summary, a type of the poet's conviction, expressed in "The Constant Symbol," that "the very words of the dictionary are a restriction to make the best of or stay out of and be silent." Frost's claim that "God's own descent / Into flesh" was intended to show the virtue of spending strongly presumes on the strength of sixty years' work, and as often in his last poems, the irony of the reduction borders on persiflage. The ostensibly Platonic description of the soul's birth in "The Trial by Existence" is likewise indebted to the Christic paradox, but less openly and hence to greater effect:

> And from a cliff top is proclaimed
>   The gathering of the souls for birth,
> The trial by existence named,
>   The obscuration upon earth.

Here, the limitation or misrepresentation Frost considered an essential feature of language is identified by means of a syntactic ambiguity with the act or process of becoming at all. The dodge centers appropriately on the rime-word "named," which may be read either as a predicate of "trial," or, by a Latinate inversion, as qualifying "existence"—the submission to language thus constituting the trial. Emerson too, in Frost's favorite poem "Uriel," likened the career of poetic speech to "the procession of the soul in matter," but Frost, at least in this early piece, makes more of its restrictive or concealing effects—of an "obscuration" derived via tradition from the spending of the preexistent Word.

Perhaps the counterpart to these passages is the vision of Faraway Meadow at the end of "The Last Mowing"—to me, the most poignant lines Frost ever wrote—in which all sense of trial is momentarily laid aside, and a wistful consummation is realized in the obviation of language:

> The place for the moment is ours
> For you, [O] tumultuous flowers,
> To go to waste and go wild in,
> All shapes and colors of flowers,
> I needn't call you by name.

The last two lines are an unusual instance of what Richard Poirier has called "negative designation"; of the way Frost's "visionary impulse . . . gets affirmed by an act of denial." For the most part, Frost would have agreed with Stevens, "All sorts of flowers. That's the sentimentalist," and it is rare to see him treating his longing—"this limitless trait in the hearts of men"— without irony. Or rather, since even here the poet's imagined moment of intimacy is ironically predicated on hearsay, it is rare to feel that despite all odds it is the longing that has triumphed.

More typical is the parodistic treatment one finds in "An Empty Threat," a deflation of the sublime in the mode of Keats's "A Song About Myself," and Thoreau's "The Old Marlborough Road." Keats, we remember, took "A Book / Full of vowels / And a shirt / With some towels . . . / And follow'd his nose to the North"—only to find the ground there as hard as in England. Thoreau, more cautious, recognized before he set out that roving was a spiritual appetite best indulged at home, that one "can get enough gravel / On the Old Marlborough Road"—though the announcement, characteristically, was only to be posted along the Road itself. Like them, Frost knows that the desire to go beyond home, to dispense with the bounds of place or the particular, is apt to confound itself unless tethered to reality. Freedom, communion, transfiguration, the lures that impel the mythical journey, are for him only vapid delusions until embodied in specific forms. His venture north to the realm of "snow and mist / That doesn't exist" in search of a fabulous father figure is thus, as his title tells us, "an empty threat" from the start:

> I stay;
> But it isn't as if . . .

The ensuing description of Hudson's Bay, despite the indicative mode, is idle fantasy, though one senses that in the canvas of Frost's oeuvre such fantasy works as a vanishing point, imposing its perspective on everything before it.

Like the brilliance of Faraway Meadow, or the mystic's cloud of unknowing to which it bears a humorous resemblance, the imagined vastness of Hudson's Bay is unobstructed by language. As a result, thought founders, and instinctual calls take the place of articulate sound. At times however, our ears play tricks on us—"The seal yelp / On an ice cake. / It's not men by some mistake?"—and we fancy ourselves perhaps in the vicinity of an Over-Soul, or on the ridge of the Alps, our rational, disjunctive light of sense usurped by the power of Imagination. To be sure, there is always a companion presence, but even he is an incarnate ambiguity:

> His name's Joe,
> Alias John,
> And between what he doesn't know
> And won't tell
> About where Henry Hudson's gone,
> I can't say he's much help;
> But we get on.

Like the *absconditus* Henry Hudson, whose secret he may or may not share, this "French Indian Esquimaux" with the double identity is a familiar, though sadly diminished, figure. As a final comment on the pretensions of unific intuition, Frost has cast him as a trapper, not of souls, but of furs—"off setting traps," which, true to tradition, he baits with his own person—"In one himself perhaps."

In sum, Hudson's Bay is a vacuous happy hunting ground, and Frost is suspicious of its infinite spaces. "Supreme merit," as he tells us in "Kitty Hawk," lies "in risking spirit / In substantiation," in sacrificing possibility for the sake of attainment. Despite the opaqueness of the medium, his ideals must be embodied and his intuitions expressed; and he leaves it to those he later labels "monists" to "end up in the universal Whole / As unoriginal as any rabbit." For the staunch individualist, absorption in this trackless au delà would constitute a defeat, a surrender to that dream of "easy gold" which he had already rejected in his early masterpiece "Mowing." There, "Anything more than the truth would have seemed too weak / To the earnest love that laid the swale in rows"—where swale is a trope for meaning, and rows for the formal constraints of language essential to its cultivation.

Nevertheless, Frost is far from impervious to the temptation he derides; for, as Poirier notes, he is at once morally committed to the necessities of form and "congenitally impatient with form and with limits." Thus, the scrupulous reservation in the last lines of "An Empty Threat" only intensifies the impression of sincere regret:

"Better defeat almost,
If seen clear,
Than life's victories of doubt
That need endless talk-talk
To make them out."

It is the dilemma of a professed "anti-Platonist," vacillating between admiration for our daedal embodiments—for the assertion of form upon chaos—and malaise at their speciousness:

At one extreme agreeing with one Greek
At the other agreeing with another Greek, . . .
A baggy figure, equally pathetic
When sedentary and when peripatetic.

["The Bear"]

II. THE SERPENT'S TALE

This deep ambivalence toward the status of the Ideal appears most tellingly in Frost's poems about women, many of whom seem to transcend their situations even as they succumb to them. I think it was Williams who once said that he never passed a homely woman without thinking of Helen of Troy. In Frost's case, the fata morgana was Eve. One suspects that at the deepest level he had identified with Milton's Adam and considered himself somehow to blame for her plight. But his fixation has a literary etiology as well; for he found in the myth of the fall the necessary premise and justification for his thoughts on concealment. Once more, one might cite the theologians, who likewise needed a fall from paradise to sustain a doctrine of incarnation.

Fallen man resigns himself with reluctance to the necessity of concealment. Like the lion's carcass, our stubborn refusal to accept dissimilation breeds its swarm of regrets and desires, nourishing the poetic urge to create a language pure enough to present ourselves intact. This urge the myth explains as our residual awareness of an unfallen state. But Frost is no Gnostic, and his work is no postlapsarian lament for lost perfection. He is willing to embrace his predicament, to entertain with earlier Stoics a notion of design. He even takes pleasure in the opportunity for self-exertion this predicament provides—a frankly pagan attitude which goes against his own Wordsworthian ideas on how poems are conceived, *sola gratia* so to speak, merrily sinning against the systematic logic of the *felix culpa*. But consistency was never Frost's hobgoblin. "You know how I am about chapter and verse," he wrote in a late letter to Victor Reichert, "somewhat irresponsible some would say. I went wielding the phrase *culpa felix* to my own purposes for a long time before I pinned myself down to what it may originally have meant in Church history."

As I have been suggesting, Frost's purposes were metaphysical as well as dramatic, and this equivocacy is reflected in his responses and allusions to the story of Eve—in its Miltonic no less than its biblical form. Since the extraterrestrial was no longer available, however, Frost was forced to localize the cosmic drama within the human part of the story. This he did by adopting the more readily camouflaged topos of the eternal feminine, or consort as muse. His heroines, like Joyce's women, remain unfallen; or rather, like Joyce's women, they remain elusive—now ideal, now vilified.

The clearest expression of this double configuration is to be found in the three "garden of Eden" poems from the section of *A Witness Tree* suggestively entitled "One or Two." The first, "The Most of It," reads like a meditation on Adam's life before Eve's creation. Everything within call is too exactly itself. There is the self, and there is the buck, the utterly other; but there is no mediating term, nothing to initiate the work of analogy and, therewith, the possibility of creative response. "Never Again Would Birds' Song Be the Same," the central leaf of the triptych, testifies to the difference made by Eve's arrival. Here the garden setting is more explicit, though Eve herself, like the ideal she represents, remains a phantasm, visible only through the eyes of the poem's grammatical subject, who is, like the poet or reader of poetry, a descendant of fallen Adam:

> He would declare and could himself believe
> That the birds there in all the garden round
> From having heard the daylong voice of Eve
> Had added to their own an oversound,
> Her tone of meaning but without the words.

In a sense, Frost's Eve is the positive counterpart of the empty threat of Hudson's Bay. As "inarticulate" as Williams's "Beautiful Thing" shimmering through the common fabric of *Paterson*, she moves in a world indifferent to names, made resonant, as the world in "The Most of It" was not, by her ineffable but musical presence. With her transforming power, she resembles too the transcendent creative principle solicited by Milton in his invocation to Urania, "The meaning, not the name, I call," a phrase echoed clearly in the fifth line of the poem. It seems to join there with the more diffused melody of Virgil's first eclogue ("Formosam resonare doces Amaryllida silvas") to mythologize the pathetic fallacy—or perhaps to mock Dr. Johnson's English translation ("And the wood rings with Amarillis' name"), for it is precisely because it is not denominative, not limed in an onomastic net, that Eve's "tone of meaning" is so all-pervasive.

Analogies to this familiar antithesis of pure and embodied meaning from the realm of poetic practice are suggested by Frost's essay, "The Figure a Poem Makes." Though the figuration is different, the alignment of the terms with revelation and concealment, or freedom and restraint, remains the same. To begin with, Frost likens the "sound" of a poem to "the gold in the ore," separable in theory though not in fact from the allegedly "inessential" contextual or verbal meaning. He then splits each of his terms in two and demonstrates the same interdependence between the halves—the conjunction of melody and meter (which recalls Milton's wedding of Voice and Verse in "At a Solemn Musick") standing to the ordering of sounds as the conjunction of "wildness" and "theme" stands to the ordering of ideas: "Just as the first mystery was how a poem could have a tune in such a straightness as meter, so the second mystery is how a poem can have wildness and at the same time a subject that shall be fulfilled." In each case, Frost conceives of the second term as imposing some limitation on the first, and the figures are all potentially metonymic for the relation of meaning and words.

In Frost's version, the fall of Eve, dramatized in the final poem of the group, will thus be represented as a fall into words. Such a development is anticipated at the end of "Never Again," where we see Eve bound for the first time by the notion of design—impressed, as it were, into the service of poetry: "And to do that to birds was why she came." The functional purpose imposed on her is less onerous perhaps than those borne by her literary sisters, but we feel it to be an outrage nonetheless. That Frost himself saw it this way is made clear by the placement of "The Subverted Flower," with its account of an actual, though abortive, impressment. I say placement, because we know from Thompson that the first draft of the poem was composed in Derry, more than thirty years before its inclusion in *A Witness Tree.* However, not only its position in the published sequence, but the parallels within the poem itself to the temptation scenes from Book Nine of *Paradise Lost* invite us to read it as a complement to the idealized vision of Eve presented in the sonnet.

Toward the end of "Never Again," the venue shifts quietly from the garden to the woods—a topographical change that subtly shadows the succession of generations and, by implication, the definitive change of aeons. At the beginning of "The Subverted Flower," Eve has already wandered outside the "garden wall" into the fallen world. The characteristic response of that world is an act of shameful self-exposure—illustrative, as I hope will be clear by now, of that purer enthusiasm, which, whether it neglect the demands of decorum or the astringencies of metaphor, inevitably ends in confusion. As usual, the analogy between sexual and poetic fruition (or frustration) looms closest, and one can trace a probable connection between Frost's attitude toward the exhibitionist in the poem and the suggestion he makes in "The Constant Symbol" that poetry "be judged for whether any original intention it had has been strongly spent or weakly lost.... Strongly spent," he concludes, "is synonymous with kept"—and to keep is to keep concealed.

It is not his will but the progressive overtness of his behavior that finally costs Eve's assailant his human dignity. As initially presented with his command of the past subjunctive, he is not only forceful but controlled, and the courtly trope that signals his desire could as well be his contrivance as the poet's:

> She drew back; he was calm:
> "It is this that had the power."
> And he lashed his open palm
> With the tender-headed flower.

Only when he relinquishes these powers of speech and indirection does the impression of crudeness take over. The flower's seed is openly spilt before the girl—and by now the trope is clearly the poet's—till we are left with the naked thing, unaccommodated man at large:

> She looked and saw the worst.
> And the dog or what it was,
> Obeying bestial laws,
> A coward save at night,
> Turned from the place and ran.
> She heard him stumble first

> And use his hands in flight.
> She heard him bark outright.

This sudden revulsion, which expresses itself as flight to cover, is, Frost would suggest, no more than the rigor of natural law against whatever ignores its preservative order—a rigor akin to that which made Milton's Adam, on waking from his first debauch to apprehend his nakedness, and in it the reality of his transgression, cry: "Cover me ye pines / Ye cedars, with innumerable boughs / Hide me...."

In Paradise the admission was consequential; in twentieth-century New England it is simply another instance of a well-established pattern. The question of the girl's role in the episode that brings about this backlash is accordingly the more interesting of the poem's two foci. At the end, of course, the man's degeneracy will redound upon her as well; yet for all the foam on her chin, she remains technically inviolate, like the Anadyomene in "Paul's Wife." In fact, the darkest implications of the poem only become apparent when we recognize that it is precisely her inviolability that brings the episode to its wretched consummation. There is nothing necessarily vicious about the man's original appeal. Rather, like the ambiguous central trope itself, it may be a prelude to fruitfulness. The degradation is gradual; and a closer look suggests that each step is precipitated by her failure to respond:

> He smiled for her to smile,
> But she was either blind
> Or willfully unkind...
> She was standing to the waist
> In goldenrod and brake,
> Her shining hair displaced.
> He stretched her either arm
> As if she made it ache
> To clasp her—not to harm;
> As if he could not spare
> To touch her neck and hair.
> "If this has come to us
> And not to me alone—"
> So she thought she heard him say;
> Though with every word he spoke
> His lips were sucked and blown
> And the effort made him choke

> Like a tiger at a bone.
> She had to lean away.

Her uncertainty about his speech is particularly significant, as it seems to mirror Eve's initial wonder, when flattered by the Serpent in *Paradise Lost*, at hearing "language of Man pronounc't / By Tongue of Brute." Indeed, the word "brute" occurs four lines later in Frost; but the image here is inverted, for it is actually the girl's reception of the broken words that puts their status as language in question. Likewise, the demeaning description of his manner of speaking, which we tend to read as her impression, antic-ipates, rather than reflects, his dehumanization. Her "shining hair" is suf-ficient to suggest a mythical or ideal beauty, which to the man who fails to appreciate its inaccessibility is potentially pernicious. It is a cold allure, and, though embodied conventionally in an image of woman, strangely akin in its fatality to that foreignness that Stevens figured more portentously in his northern lights. It too can be seen as the serpent's nest, the poetic equivalent of evil's source, "responsible" for educing what Emerson has called the "tragedy of incapacity." Thus, the ominous opening words of the poem, "She drew back,"reverberate, once the catastrophe is sure, in indictment of the girl:

> A girl could only see
> That a flower had marred a man,
> But what she could not see
> Was that the flower might be
> Other than base and fetid:
> That the flower had done but part,
> And what the flower began
> Her own too meager heart
> Had terribly completed.

Of course, the very venture beyond the garden wall into the wild field of flowers was already an invitation to trouble. In Milton's poem, Adam reproaches Eve with "that strange / Desire of wand'ring," and throughout Frost's work the same figure is used to signify that "extra-vagant" longing for perfect freedom which if not restrained brings inevitable calamity. In first-person poems like "Into My Own," "The Sound of Trees," "An Empty Threat," "Stopping by Woods," "Come In," and many more, the poet himself wisely resists this longing—either by subordinating it as contrary to fact or relegating it to an indefinite future—but the women in the nar-ratives are often less circumspect. The foreboding that one feels for the wife

at the door in "Home Burial" or for the wife in "A Servant to Servants,"
who could "Drop everything and live out on the ground," is justified by
the effect of the fugitive daughter's extravagance in "The Housekeeper,"
and more terribly by the fate of the woman in "The Hill Wife," who on a
sudden "impulse" wanders from the loneliness of a barren marriage to a
solitude beyond bound or bourn:

> She rested on a log and tossed
>   The fresh chips,
> With a song only to herself
>   On her lips.
>
> And once she went to break a bough
>   Of black alder.
> She strayed so far she scarcely heard
>   When he called her—
>
> And didn't answer—didn't speak—
>   Or return.

The emphasis on reticence here is typical; for it is their reluctance to
compromise themselves with words that gives to so many of Frost's heroines
the air of innocence or of nobility incommensurate with the meanness of
their lives. By the same token, so long as she keeps silent, the girl in "The
Subverted Flower" manages, despite the poet's indictment, to preserve a
virginal purity. Unlike the woman in "The Hill Wife," however, she is alert
to the call from home—to the repercussions of her absence if not of her
presence—and so, in the end, as her passage from pregnant silence to sterile
and profane speech makes manifest, her purity perishes while she survives.
This passage is carefully anticipated by an awakening of her other senses,
corresponding to the simultaneous decline in the man's speech and sight
(note that at the end he stumbles and has to "use his hands in flight"). Thus,
whereas she begins as if "blind" and with uncertain hearing ("she thought
she heard him say"), in the second half of the poem she actively "looks,"
"sees," or "hears" in five successive sentences before—with Eve, her eyes
how opened, and her mind how darkened—she finally accedes to her own
voice:

> And oh, for one so young
> The bitter words she spit
> Like some tenacious bit
> That will not leave the tongue.

> She plucked her lips for it,
> And still the horror clung.
> Her mother wiped the foam
> From her chin, picked up her comb
> And drew her backward home.

The irony is that this accession is itself a decline. Language here is compared to a "bit"—a restraint unknown to the "tiger at a bone," but alien too, to Eve in Paradise. Just as the man's flight and submersion in animality were fit retribution for his presumptive self-exposure, so this figurative curb requites the young Eve for her provocative will to wander. Again, one is reminded of Milton's lines: "restraint she will not brook, / And left to herself, if evil thence ensue, / She first his weak indulgence will accuse." To complete the parallel only two things need be added: that her outburst merits pity as well as reproof, and that the responsibility for the evil wrought is mutual.

In *Paradise Lost*, where the ultimate responsibility for evil—for the struggle between passion and reason (or freedom and restraint)—lies outside the human sphere altogether, this second point is less salient. Given the reality of the angelic order, Milton was able to construct a noncommutative chain of influence with Eve, both tempted and tempting, in the center, and the Serpent and Adam at either end (though the fact that Adam initiates their dalliance after the fall doubtless anticipates a new reciprocity). For Frost, however, responsibility is confined to the human sphere, and temptation is thus viciously reciprocal from the start. If Adam is tempted, Eve must be the temptress, *and* vice versa. Although narrative devices and interpolated comments challenging the more obvious reading of the incident both tend to exonerate the man, his culpability is reestablished at a deeper level by the structural parallels between his progress and that of Milton's Tempter: for example, that both prosper through ambiguity until their intentions are realized, or that both then abandon human speech and withdraw. There is Miltonic precedent too for the way Frost aligns perception with speech and uses them to create the chiastic pattern in which the tempter's powers wane as the tempted's revive.

In the end, both masculine and feminine narrative lines circle back on themselves and interlock, until there is no way of telling whether the "subverted flower" of the title is the girl or the man, or simply the prospect of coalescence represented by the nameless flowers of Faraway Meadow. In place of that prospect, we are given a cage of moral ambiguities, reminiscent of the mirrored boxes of Hawthorne or Henry James, whose paradise-lost view of reality Frost shares, as he shares their fascination with emblems and their insistence on craftsmanship. He shares too their respectful impatience with Emerson, of whom he once wrote in criticism that "he could see the 'good of evil born' but he couldn't bring himself to say the evil of good born." If we accept the inaccessible girl with the shining hair as another embodiment of the beautiful thing, then the tale of degradation Frost here tells so powerfully brings that criticism to life.

Admittedly, this sequence of poems shows Frost at his most dialectical. For the most part, the women in the narrative poems have long since been requited for their kinship with Eve, and rather than obscure them further, Frost prefers to let them shine as they can. Despite their subject or "fallen" state—generally suggested by the bond of marriage or economic dependence—their speech and vision tend to remain chaste. At its extreme, this chastity threatens to become a cutting-off of all relation, as when the wife in "Home Burial," convinced of her husband's inner blindness, rejects his attempts at rapprochement and, in a line that recalls the conclusion of "Paul's Wife," forbids him to even mention their buried child:

> [He:] "A man can't speak of his own child that's dead."

> [She:] "You can't because you don't know how to speak."

But usually it is more benevolent: the granddaughter in "The Generations of Men" simply "using her eyes" to read the true profile of the stranger beside her, or the wife in "West-Running Brook" responding with a name to the gay wave in the stream on which her husband discourses. It is as though the poisoned fruit which destroyed their hopes had left their desires still pure, so that they themselves might become a source of nourishment. To be sure, the "sound of meaning" is now all but inaudible. As the wife "with a houseful of hungry men to feed" admits in "A Servant to Servants":

> There's nothing but a voice-like left inside
> That seems to tell me how I ought to feel,
> And would feel if I wasn't all gone wrong

—for she is as tightly confined by life's contingencies as her mad uncle was by his hickory cage. Yet for all their obscurity, they are never devious or indirect, but remain—if only by their passive endurance—priestesses of the Ideal. One might call them hobbled transcendentalists, or remembering their potential balefulness, follow Frost's wrier lead and dub them witches, who though perched between two worlds—as the Pauper Witch of Grafton between her battling towns—must in the end, along with Eve, "come down from everything to nothing."

III. THE LONGEST WAY ROUND

The fall from Eden, like the fall of the tower of Babel, was a fall into confusion. The late poem "Directive," which ends with an invitation to "Drink and be whole again beyond confusion," has usually been read as Frost's program for a poetic sacrament that would carry us beyond our fallen state. However, the text bristles with warnings that should caution us against accepting its apparent assertions too quickly. Of these, the most striking is the allusion to St. Mark which immediately precedes the conclusion. The symbolic itinerary has been completed, and the poet has brought us to his rustic equivalent of the eternal source or waters of life:

> I have kept hidden in the instep arch
> Of an old cedar at the waterside
> A broken drinking goblet like the Grail
> Under a spell so the wrong ones can't find it,
> So can't get saved, as Saint Mark says they mustn't.

The patent reference is to the lines following the parable of the sower, in which Jesus is represented as expounding the necessity of concealment: "And he said unto them, Unto you it is given to know the mystery of the kingdom of God: but unto them that are without, all these things are done in parables: That seeing they may see, and not perceive; and hearing they may hear, and not understand...." An allusion to the same passage in the roughly contemporaneous essay "A Romantic Chasm" makes it clear that for Frost the outsiders or "wrong ones" are those who lack the patience or dexterity to follow that constant "word-shift by metaphor" which keeps the language of poetry from ever meaning simply what it says.

Elitist postures can be exasperating, and it may be argued that "Directive," like the other blank-verse narratives in which the "I" dissociates itself didactically from the reader ("New Hampshire," "The White-Tailed Hornet"), ends up imposing its purpose rather than "discovering" it the way Frost says a good poem should. Nevertheless, the prerogatives Frost is claiming here are not his own but, as in the tower of Babel letter where he identifies himself with God, those which the mystery of poetry enjoins on its initiates. Moreover, the very flagrance of his posing is our clue that it hides an underlying motive. As should be clear by now, Frost's allusions are far subtler than those flaunted vermiculations to which the "more difficult" modernists have accustomed us. In the case of "Directive," I believe the poetic target is Wordsworth's *Excursion*, and the scriptural stalking-horse is intended simultaneously to publish and to disguise its presence.

This double function begins with the mention of the Grail; for Frost's "broken goblet" is meant to redeem the "useless fragment of a wooden bowl, / Green with the moss of years," which the Wanderer finds by the hidden spring in Book One of Wordsworth's poem. Wordsworth's fragment is "useless" in that the Wanderer will not drink from it. Instead it becomes the focus of the elegiac impulse that dominates this part of the work; a figure, more tentative than the Boy of Winander whom it anticipates, for the poetic self in the obligatory act of dying vicariously in order to be reborn. Echoes of the Wordsworthian dialectic are clearest in the opening lines of Frost's poem, where explicitly elegiac gestures—unless read tongue-in-cheek as the subsequent lapse in diction invites—prepare us for an excursion along the *via negativa*:

> Back out of all this now too much for us,
> Back in a time made simple by the loss
> Of detail, burned, dissolved, and broken off
> Like graveyard marble sculpture in the weather,
> There is a house that is no more a house
> Upon a farm that is no more a farm
> And in a town that is no more a town.

From *Lycidas* to Stevens's dirge for the tropical planter in *Notes toward a Supreme Fiction*, such secularized paradox is at the heart of the sublime tradition in English and American poetry. Frost, however, is a poet of "counter-love," for whom the supreme fiction has not to be imagined but discovered—and not in ostentatious isolation, but working "whether together or apart" in inevitable league with others. He thus revises the Wordsworthian itinerary by putting the fragment to use. To speak in parables, the bowl outside Wordsworth's ruined cottage resembles the corn of wheat that must die in order to bear; the broken goblet in Frost, like the faithful servant's talent, is a counter for pragmatic exchange.

Like the Gospel parables themselves, "Directive" can be read in two ways. It can be interpreted point for point (allegorically); or it can be construed in its entirety as illustrating a single conviction (the way form criticism insists Jesus' parables were originally meant to be taken). The latter approach suggests an alternative to the sacramental reading of the poem; for search as we may, the only integrating conviction—the only common term between Frost's poem and experience—is the certainty of fragmentation. That is, read as parable, the poem invites us to achieve the only wholeness possible by becoming reconciled to the imperfect. It offers us a road—later called a ladder—that "may seem as if it should have been a quarry," glacial etchings in the rock, cellar holes, a field eroded to the size of a harness gall, and, in its midst, a "children's house of make-believe," with some "shattered dishes" and the broken goblet used to draw the water. These analects become more meaningful when read with an eye to their individual histories—especially in Frost's own poems. Thus, if we move to an "allegorical" reading, the "ladder road" recalls the two-pointed ladder of metaphor that points toward heaven in "After Apple-Picking"; the glacier "that braced his feet against the Arctic Pole" is a manifestation or emissary of the same elusive unnameable that haunts the polar mind in "An Empty Threat"; and the traces it leaves on the ledges run "southeast-northwest" by reason of the same imaginative westering that makes all "zest / To materialize / By on-penetration" run in the same direction in "Kitty Hawk."

This fragmentary style of reference seems especially fitting in a poem that would vindicate process. As Frost writes in "The Prerequisites," "A poem is best read in the light of all the other poems ever written. We read A the better to read B. . . . Progress is not the aim, but circulation." Moreover, his determination in "The Lesson for Today," to "take [his] incompleteness with the rest," shows that he recognized the limitations of the approach. And yet a close explicator could still argue that the aim of "Directive" is to transcend and so perfect its fragments: that the counterplot I have been tracing is only its *praeparatio evangelica*. The final question is thus whether "the road there," so similar to the dialectical path of the quest romance, leads to some determinate source, or whether our gift at journey's end is just the preacher's vexing wisdom. Does one really come back to the original word or only to another departure?

The answer hinges on our reading of the final phrase, "beyond confusion." The word "confusion" occurs frequently in Frost's work, where it usually connotes disorder and defeat. The reference to the confusion of Babel in Frost's letter to Cox, for example, and the description of "the background in hugeness and confusion shading away from where we stand into black and utter chaos" in his letter to *The Amherst Student* both depend on this usage. If this is the only sense intended in "Directive," then the final line exceeds without question Frost's own definition of a poem's end as "a momentary stay against confusion." The invitation to "drink and be whole again" would be a call to unmediated vision—a call to ascend from Babel not by the two-pointed ladder of metaphor, but directly. But "confusion" may have another meaning, as exemplified in the final line of Frost's early poem "Rose Pogonias:"

> We raised a simple prayer
> Before we left the spot,

That in the general mowing
    That place might be forgot;
Or if not all so favored,
    Obtain such grace of hours
That none should mow the grass there
    While so confused with flowers.

Here Frost, the student of Latin poetry, is punning on the etymologically prior sense of blending or fusing together in the manner of Milton, for whom the original sense of a Latinate word often points back toward an unfallen world ("with mazy error," "sapient fruit"). Allowing that the same etymological play is active in the final line of "Directive," Frost's invitation to wholeness is qualified by an antithetical intimation that the only wholeness or health we can know is to be free from the illusory ideal of perfection—to accept, with full knowledge of its inadequacy, the wisdom of concealment and restraint.

A similar ambiguity is active in Job's lines from *A Masque of Reason*, written about the same time:

Yet I suppose what seems to us confusion
Is not confusion, but the form of forms,
The serpent's tail stuck down the serpent's throat,
Which is the symbol of eternity.

One thinks in reading them of Coleridge's remark to Joseph Cottle (7 March 1815) that "the common end of all *narrative*, nay, of *all* Poems, is to convert a series into a *Whole*: to make those events, which in real or imagined History move on a strait Line, assume to our Understandings a *circular* motion—the snake with its Tail in its Mouth." Yet presumably there is an undercurrent in Frost's version that links it to the unconverted and unconverting circles of Emerson's "Uriel," the "greatest Western [i.e., American] poem yet," as Job goes on immediately to say. My own conclusion is that within the context of Frost's poem Job is a weak reader whose word must be completed by that of his wife (Thyatira, after the New Testament city famed for its witches), who knows the world as the "hard place" where man "can try himself / And find out whether he is any good." For Frost, the "tail stuck down the serpent's throat" is the tale Eve swallowed in the garden, the false promise of a prematurely perfected vision. In eternity, perhaps, Uriel's cry will be heard, the series will be converted, and the circle will focus to a single point. In the meantime, that symbol remains a figure; for the fruit that brought the dualities of good and evil to Eve and her descendants also brought duplicity—the coats of skins—and metaphor to bind them together.

"There is throughout nature," wrote Emerson, "something mocking, something that leads us on and on. . . . We live in a system of approximations. Every end is prospective of some other end." "Directive" is a parable of hermeneutic circulation. True, the search for understanding must begin with our initial faith that some sense is there to be discovered: that *la dive bouteille* when pieced together will not be found empty. But what if we find it half-empty? And if so, should we call it half-empty or half-full? That, to recall a teacher's words, was the oven bird's dilemma—the "diminished thing" and what to make of it. The traditional reading of "Directive" approaches it from the half-full side, as a parable of sufficiency, an affirmation of the power of poetry to embody real meanings in which the properly initiated may happily come to share. It makes the hermeneutical circle a sacramental *temenos*, a magic precinct where source and terminus coalesce. But it misses the critical ambiguity. A reading that achieves its source can only be an icon or an artifact. Frost's sovereign principle of metaphor is, on the contrary, a machine for displacement, and every attained meaning must redeem a correspondent loss.

Late in his career, Frost recounted the history of his own lifelong engagement to this hard truth in a narrative poem, "The Discovery of the Madeiras," and placed it at the end of "One or Two." For all its apparent urbanity, the story of the fugitive lovers has the terrible rigor of a sphinx's riddle; for the interpolated tale of the slave couple sacrificed on the high seas is really a parable of the lovers' own fate. Their responses to the oracle differ, however: she withdraws from its harshness, and, constant to some incommunicable ideal, dies "of thought" on a nameless island; he, more bold, dares to conceive it, and so sails on, having buried her there and written, as marriage lines, an epitaph. In the end, his gesture is naturally misread: the island is named for him, not for her. But that, as Frost tells us, is "neither here nor there"; for history too is a choice of figments.

CHARLES BERGER

Echoing Eden: Frost and Origins

Of the major modern poets, Frost seems the least driven to create myths or fictions of origin, the least prone to mystify beginnings. He will have nothing to do with the sacred investiture of the past, whether historical or autobiographical. He resembles Stevens in the belief that the sense "of cold and earliness is a daily sense, / Not the predicate of bright origin" ("An Ordinary Evening in New Haven"), but does not share Stevens's obsession with finding first ideas apart from authoritarian first principles. Though Frost is most profoundly an exploratory poet, whose work indeed *is* knowing, as Richard Poirier's title tells us, he would not hymn the search for the ground of such knowing as Stevens does: "To re-create, to use / The cold and earliness and bright origin / Is to search." Frost privileges neither the constructed locus of origin nor the search for it with Stevens' high eloquence. At the same time, one cannot read through Frost's poetry and fail to notice how many of his poems engage, however playfully or skeptically, those issues we group under the figurative heading of "origins," even to the point of his invoking Eden and the Fall to describe ongoing moments in consciousness. In his poems of brooks, pools, and gardens, in his speculations on the wellsprings of sound and song, Frost shows an uncanny ability to approach the formerly sacred source, to broach the beginning of things, without yielding to their hieratic lure. Frost plays upon the prestige of these themes, but ends by including or accommodating them within, not outside, the range of lyric discursiveness. His poetic intelligence thrives on the recognition that all beginnings are fictions.

Published for the first time in this volume. © 1986 by Charles Berger.

A good example of how Frost can play with the subject of beginnings comes in a little-discussed poem called "The Valley's Singing Day":

> The sound of the closing outside door was all.
> You made no sound in the grass with your footfall,
> As far as you went from the door, which was not far;
> But you had awakened under the morning star
> The first songbird that awakened all the rest.
> He could have slept but a moment more at best.
> Already determined dawn began to lay
> In place across a cloud the slender ray
> For prying beneath and forcing the lids of sight,
> And loosing the pent-up music of overnight.
> But dawn was not to begin their "pearly-pearly"
> (By which they mean the rain is pearls so early,
> Before it changes to diamonds in the sun),
> Neither was song that day to be self-begun.
> You had begun it, and if there needed proof—
> I was asleep still under the dripping roof,
> My window curtain hung over the sill to wet;
> But I should awake to confirm your story yet;
> I should be willing to say and help you say
> That once you had opened the valley's singing day.

This remarkably subtle poem avoids claiming too much for the action it describes, while at the same time showing how easy—how natural—it would be to magnify such an incident. The teasing enjambment of the fourth line makes us first take "awakened" as intransitive (helped in this by the poetical "under the morning star"), accustomed as we are to the heightened rhetoric of beginnings. As we read on, we discover that the action can be explained a little less hyperbolically; something has been jarred from sleep, simply awakened by a nearly inaudible sound. But the initial suggestion roused in us will not entirely disappear and the identification of the bird as "the first" perhaps keeps us within an enlarged sphere of possibility.

But the poem scales down to anecdote, to "story," as if to imply that all accounts of beginnings or awakenings contain their share of arbitrariness or accident. The comedy of disproportion here arises from the gap between effort and effect: so little goes into achieving what might be regarded, in another poem, as so much. Placing oneself at the dawn, inserting oneself at the opening of day so that song would not be "self-begun" but originated by an outside, prevenient presence, this sounds like the plot of a revised hymn to sunrise—but of a different poem, as well. These "larger" themes are echoed playfully throughout this singing day's valley. But it would not be play, as Frost says elsewhere, were it not for mortal stakes.

The dialectical complement of Frost's wary attraction to original sites and sounds may be discovered in his many poems about *echo*. Its obvious associations with pastoralism matter less for the interpreter of Frost than the use of echo as a figure for repetition and reflection (to bring in the visual analogue). Frost's poetry complicates the hierarchical opposition between the fullness of original sound and the faintness of echo. If he does not go all the way toward regarding repetition as mastery or originality, he certainly avoids seeing it as diminution. A central distinction made by John Hollander in *The Figure of Echo* between echo and allusion helps to explain Frost's attitude toward verbal repetition:

> We might, indeed, propose a kind of rhetorical hierarchy for the relationship of allusive modes. Actual *quotation*, the literal presence of a body of text, is represented or replaced by *allusion*, which may be fragmentary or periphrastic. In the case of outright allusion ... the text alluded to is not totally absent, but is part of the portable library shared by the author and his ideal audience. Intention to allude recognizably is essential to the concept. ... But then there is echo, which represents or substitutes for allusion as allusion does for quotation. ... In contrast with literary allusion, echo is a metaphor of, and for, alluding, and does not depend on conscious intention.

By these criteria, Frost would certainly have to be considered a poet of echo rather than allusion. Echo is less referential and intentional than allusion, while at the same time being more figurative. Rather than calling attention to a particular passage, it makes the reader aware of temporality in its pure state. Echo acknowledges indebtedness by figuratively indicating the temporality of the poet's discourse, but works to free that dependence from association with the notion of poetic property, thereby easing the burden of belatedness. Frost's concept of "sentence sounds," preexisting patterns of sound belonging to the genius of the language, amounts to just such a theory of echoing:

> They are apprehended by the ear. They are gathered by the ear from the vernacular and brought into books. Many of them are already familiar to us in books. I think no writer invents them.

The most original writer only catches them fresh from talk, where
they grow spontaneously.

No critic writing today would have any difficulty exposing the ideali-
zations of this passage, its accordance of priority to speech over writing, or
its natural analogues for the process of composition: sounds, which "grow
spontaneously" in nature, are gathered (as are crops) or caught (as are animals). Frost himself leaves it an open question as to whether we apprehend
sentence sounds from talk or from books. But priority is not really the issue
here. What matters for Frost is that the poet capture what Marie Borroff, in
her study of Frost's language, terms "native" dialect, the strength of the vernacular. Such a concept seems to fuse origin and echo, insofar as the quest
for the vernacular always implies a figurative return to "authentic" language,
language at the source, "first" words. But this return also involves a repetition, since the vernacular keeps such language alive and in circulation. It
might be said that for Frost the ideal of the native stands in for the stricter
sense of the origin that one encounters in other poets. A poem such as "Hyla
Brook"—"our brook," as Frost calls it—with its refusal to pursue the stream
underground in a quest for the deep source, typifies this attitude. The reso-
nances of native speech represent an accommodated purity, for Frost is not
the poet of the still center. Poirier distinguishes Frost from some of the romantics in that he does not regard human consciousness as a burden. I would
also add that, as opposed to some of his nearer contemporaries, he does not
regard the inherently figurative nature of language to be a burden either, and
so does not seek radical cures for the imprecisions of language.

In what follows, I will be considering a series of poems on the subject
of origins and echoes. These poems should give a strong sense of the different
guises under which this central concern appears in Frost. I hesitate to call
it an obsession, since that word does not square with the subtlety of Frost's
artistry. Although the sequence I have chosen ends with "Directive"—a
poem that ends a number of other essays on Frost—I do not intend that
poem to be regarded as a culmination, or summa, of Frost's thinking on
the subject. Frost's *oeuvre* is the most decentered of any major, modern
poet and for the critic to construct a central poem would be to violate the
sceptical integrity of his work. All these poems echo each other, in their
strategies of covering and recovering the origin.

I

"The Aim Was Song" begins, "Before man came"—but nothing in
Frost's rhetoric suggests that he wishes to capture the accents of this pre-

historic, prelinguistic moment. Frost does not mystify the subject of "Before man"; indeed, it remains for him a subject, capable of being declaimed upon along with other subjects. Frost does not try to use language to express the epoch *before* language. Poetic primitivism is not his way:

> Before man came to blow it right
>   The wind once blew itself untaught,
> And did its loudest day and night
>   In any rough place where it caught.
>
> Man came to tell it what was wrong:
>   It hadn't found the place to blow;
> It blew too hard—the aim was song.
>   And listen—how it ought to go!
>
> He took a little in his mouth,
>   And held it long enough for north
> To be converted into south,
>   And then by measure blew it forth.
>
> By measure. It was word and note,
>   The wind the wind had meant to be—
> A little through the lips and throat.
>   The aim was song—the wind could see.

Scattered throughout the poem are teasingly moral terms, such as "right," "wrong," and "ought." The wind itself must be taught. And yet these moral terms have an aesthetic basis to them: "measure" is not so much a moral as an aesthetic category. Learning to measure and order the instrument means learning to play it right, learning to find the smooth as opposed to the rough places. Civilization is a form of measure. Morality might sneak in here in the sense that there is a guiding principle to the search for measure. That is, Frost may be implying that moral systems grow out of a deep-seated, instinctual urge for measure and order, a need on our part to convert things to human scale.

The process of turning undifferentiated wind into the measures of "word and note" involves an act of conversion—"North . . . converted into south"—a turning of the wind against itself, so to speak. Wind is drawn in and then returned as the exhalation of song. Insofar as song is composed partly of natural wind, it is mimetic, a point Frost makes through the mirroring of the word in the line, "The wind the wind had meant to be." But nature is also changed by song's superaddition of meaning, even if such a gesture works to restore a sense of natural mimesis by ascribing a similar meaning to nature itself. In his half-jocular way, Frost stands the Wordsworthian model of nature as pedagogue on its head, by having man become the instructor. The lesson learned, "the wind could see."

The conversion of natural wind into song marks a triumph of human scale and meaning. Sound is converted into song through a twisting or a wrenching, a turning of strength inside out. In making of the wind a human song, we thereby create a sense of order: the measures of song precede the measures of law. If the aim is song, then to be wrong is to misaim, to hit the wrong note, the wrong target, to be guilty of *hamartia*.

"Sitting by a Bush in Broad Sunlight" has drawn surprisingly little comment from the critics, as if its underlying complexities were only too readily translated by confident artistry. The poem's tetrameter couplets invoke Emerson's oracular meter, but the trumpeting is muted here, the line more flexible. The poem's overt subject is entropy, the decline from fire to mere warmth, with the specter of winter not far removed:

> When I spread out my hand here today,
> I catch no more than a ray
> To feel of between thumb and fingers;
> No lasting effect of it lingers.
>
> There was one time and only the one
> When dust really took in the sun;
> And from that one intake of fire
> All creatures still warmly suspire.
>
> And if men have watched a long time
> And never seen sun-smitten slime
> Again come to life and crawl off,
> We must not be too ready to scoff.
>
> God once declared He was true
> And then took the veil and withdrew,
> And remember how final a hush
> Then descended of old on the bush.
>
> God once spoke to people by name.
> The sun once imparted its flame.
> One impulse persists as our breath;
> The other persists as our faith.

Though the poem is startlingly literal in its declaration that "There was one time and only the one," Frost displays little sense of loss, little elegiac lament. To state the terms of decline so baldly is perhaps to expose the impossibility of the original moment—that "one time"— from which we appear to have fallen. Sentences such as "God once spoke to people by name," or "The sun once imparted its flame," are possible only because of "once," the signifier of irrecoverable priority. "Once" marks the precincts of *illo tempore*, the sacred space of story time, of origin conceived as a story. Throughout the poem, Frost threatens to convert these absolute statements into terms of wit, thereby bringing the sacred into the social realm. The act of spreading out "here today" takes priority over the loss of elemental fire. Frost is able both to describe his inability to catch fire, to "take" in the sun, and his inability to mourn the loss of such elemental power.

"Sitting by a Bush in Broad Sunlight" is balanced between scoffing tones and tones of awe, between the coyness of "God...took the veil and withdrew," and the imagining of a moment when "dust really took in the sun," a moment when it was possible to catch fire from the source of fire. Frost also plays with two creation stories here, one divine, one natural: the spark of genesis comes from God's Word, it comes from the sun's flames. I have deliberately omitted "or" from the last clause, for the two accounts need not be competing ones. Frost has united the images of speech and fire as we find them in the story of the burning bush. God's speech issues in fire: prophetic or pentecostal speech. Frost's poem has no real room for speculation on this kind of speech, nor does Frost do so elsewhere in his poetry, but he gives us a glimpse of such a conjunction in this poem. Frost assumes that we are separated from such fiery speech, just as we are separated from the truth, once declared but now withdrawn, and he does not mourn the loss of such verbal immediacy. The poem's opening line presents an image of the hand as an emblem of artistic technique and Frost chooses it over the burning tongue of prophetic discourse. Along these same lines, he reveals himself to be a watcher, not a seer: "And if men have watched a long time / And never seen...."

The act of sitting by a bush in broad sunlight is, of course, a pale echo of Moses' stance before the burning bush; Frost's speaker is more like Mordechai before the palace gates. Frostian wit, the power of his epigrammatic style, tempers both the pain of loss and quizzes the reality of the supposed lost object. The last stanza of the poem makes it clear that Frost is interested primarily in what he calls our persistence: this is his strong word for echoing, repetition, continuation. The last lines rhyme "faith" and "breath"—though they are the most pronounced off-rhymes in the poem—

but the possibility of chiastic structuring makes it impossible to assign these terms with certainty to either sun or God. Does our breath derive from God's speech or the sun's flame? Fire has been allied with suspiration throughout the poem, so it might be natural to assume that the sun's imparted gift still persists as our breath. God's speech, then, is our faith. But these terms could just as easily be reversed. Is breath stronger than faith? And, if so, is it stronger because it comes from nature and not God?

II

The conjunction of green and gold in "Nothing Gold Can Stay" merges myths of the garden and the golden age, while also introducing, through "gold," an artificial note into the account. *Firstness*, Frost seems to say, has an unnatural cast to it.

> Nature's first green is gold,
> Her hardest hue to hold.
> Her early leaf's a flower;
> But only so an hour.
> Then leaf subsides to leaf.
> So Eden sank to grief,
> So dawn goes down to day.
> Nothing gold can stay.

The ability to distinguish a green that differs from itself, a green that is gold, argues an artificial perspective—the Yeatsian "artifice of eternity"— that can only momentarily be held, whether in Nature or the poet's mind. Such a distinction is doomed to slip away or be elided, a process the poem enacts through the grammatical elision of "Her early leaf's a flower." At the same time, the natural process of growth and expansion is implicated in the loss of earliness to a grosser lateness. What one scale of measurement registers as growth, another sees as loss, diminution, entropic dwindling. The sense of a Fall, made explicit throughout in words such as "sank" and "goes down," is also reinforced by the dominant falling rhythm of the trochaic line. When the word "grief" enters the poem, it has the force of "misery" in Stevens's "The Snow Man," a word which reveals the human reverberations of this apparently impersonal process.

But the loss is not absolute, for the poem proffers a counter-cycle of repetitive restitution. Dawn goes down today but will rise again tomorrow. The hour will again come round. The final line becomes the poem's title and undoes finality by beginning the poem over again. The last line goes down in order to come up again, like the sun. Echoing the title, it takes on the force of a refrain, a daily dirge rather than an epitaph. The first idea, as Stevens says in "Notes toward a Supreme Fiction," comes and goes, comes and goes, all day. Golden vision yields to the day's green going. Art itself is synecdochal, an hour to a day, but an hour that is guaranteed, even as it cannot be prolonged.

"These pools," the emblematic focus of meditation in "Spring Pools," are curiously double in nature: conceived as wellsprings or sources, they nevertheless reflect as well as generate. And in this reflection they do not lose or diminish that which they reflect. If we regard reflection as the visual equivalent of echo, then what is reflected (echoed) is given back nearly in its entirety, or its totality, as Frost puts it: "These pools that, though in forests, still reflect / The total sky almost without defect." So the spring pools, as first idea, as picture of nature in the cleanliness of the first idea, is already a reflection. Derrida might be invoked here, in a comment upon the impossibility of simple unity even at the point or place of origin: "There are no simple origins, for what is reflected is split *in itself* and not only as an addition to itself of its image; the reflection, the image, the double, splits what it doubles." If we privilege the pools as "clear" or "invisible" ink, linked to inner sight, over the darkening scrawl of the summer trees, then we need to remember that the pools are not a transparency but a reflection.

The sense of doubling, or narcissistic reflection culminates in the image of "flowery waters and watery flowers." The doubling of self through reflection is set against the doubling or extension of self through biological propagation, as in the generative power of the trees to produce leaves. It is not a question of poetry being more like one paradigm than the other, more narcissistic than generative; rather, poetry is both at the same time. The poem tricks us into thinking that one phase yields to the other, as early spring to summer, in a mimesis of natural process. Keats said that if poetry comes not as easily as leaves to the tree, it had better not come at all, but poetry also comes as easily as Narcissus to his image. In many poems, Frost is only too willing to align poetry with so-called "natural" generation, but here he reminds us that poetry is also a cold pastoral, fixed on itself, a power not to be used for something else.

The same idea of a cold paradise can be found in "A Winter Eden," another cold pastoral in which the ideal moment proves curiously sexless. The poem combines much of the thinking found in "Nothing Gold Can Stay" and "Spring Pools," but it is a more animated, playful poem. By the calendar of its emblematic setting, "A Winter Eden" takes place earlier than "Spring Pools"; snow remains unmelted, the hibernating trees do not start from their winter sleep:

> A winter garden in an alder swamp,
> Where conies now come out to sun and romp,
> As near a paradise as it can be
> And not melt snow or start a dormant tree.
>
> It lifts existence on a plane of snow
> One level higher than the earth below,
> One level nearer heaven overhead,
> And last year's berries shining scarlet red.
>
> It lifts a gaunt luxuriating beast
> Where he can stretch and hold his highest feast
> On some wild apple-tree's young tender bark,
> What well may prove the year's high girdle mark.

In the great line "So near to paradise all pairing ends," Frost, with the grave whimsy he manages so well, imagines a point at which the marriage-duty ends and, along with it, the duty to be a poet of marriage:

> So near to paradise all pairing ends:
> Here loveless birds now flock as winter friends,
> Content with bud-inspecting. They presume
> To say which buds are leaf and which are bloom.

Whereas "Spring Pools" emphasized a chilly narcissism, "A Winter Eden" plays up the sportiveness of its scene. In both poems the moment itself is valued, as opposed to anything it might induce, even though the "hour of winter day" is shadowed throughout by knowledge of its brevity. The poem's couplets—its "double knock," to use the phrasing of the last stanza—keep this sense of closure before us at all points, culminating in the dirge-like "This Eden day is done at two o'clock." Though such a day is short, we find no sense here that "Eden sank to grief." Not the fruit, but the bark of the "wild apple tree" is eaten; perhaps the absence of marriage sets a limit to disobedience. Frost contrives a language of innocence in "A Winter Eden," in which words such as "romp" and "sport" seem to find their proper place, salvaged from the bin of anachronism by inclusion in a deliberately anachronistic scene, as any return to Eden must be.

III

"The Most of It" presents us with yet another version of the American Adam, our native solitary, willfully establishing himself in a wilderness Eden and echoing Adam's lament over lack of suitable companionship. Poirier is right to point out the absurdity of imagining a dramatic situation here, but surely Frost has nevertheless drawn a recognizable character, however allegorical. And this character, as is often the case in lyric, is a narrower consciousness than its author, distorted through exaggeration. The outrageous presumption of the opening line—"He thought he kept the universe alone"—dwindles into the foibles of an Adamic literalist, one who would go about "recreating" the original story, who would literally place himself in Adam's position in order perhaps to experience the inauguration of a new "counter-love, original response":

> He thought he kept the universe alone;
> For all the voice in answer he could wake
> Was but the mocking echo of his own
> From some tree-hidden cliff across the lake.
> Some morning from the boulder-broken beach
> He would cry out on life, that what it wants
> Is not its own love back in copy speech,
> But counter-love, original response.

Voice calls to voice here, but the solitary receives a debased echo, an echo described as "mocking." This is not a tautological description; other forms of echo abound and the poetic tradition, not to mention Frost's poetry, is filled with them. This echo validates nothing. It issues from a source that remains hidden, a "tree-hidden cliff;" within the cliff, perhaps there is a cave, a hidden mouth. This mocking voice bounces off the cliff-side, not from out of the oracular voice of caves.

The satire here, among numerous possibilities, is that this American Adam should seek an "original response," while remaining himself such a literalist of the original story. A copy himself, he hopes to break the mold. His delusion is to think that by copying Adam he will raise the copy of Eve, another Eve. But though he disclaims any narcissistic motive (and is mocked by Echo), I think that readers can decipher the self-aggrandizing mode of one who thinks he keeps the universe alone. For this character is only self-sponsored; he enters on no colloquy, such as the original Adam. Yet he is also too weak to glory in his solipsism, for perhaps at bottom he realizes that it is indeed derivative. Raising echoes, he himself is an echo. Without

the strength either to imagine a fit companion or actually summon the
embodiment of his desire, his cry trails off into pathos. The humor in "The
Most of It" comes from a weak poet figure placing himself in a situation
where impossible strength is required, the strength either to persist in one's
own delusion and crown it with the honorific "imagination," or to seduce
another into sharing one's solitude. Both solipsism and relationship are
equally beyond this crier's powers. Unlike the married solitaries in Frost's
earlier narrative poems, he generates no dialogue.

The joke played on him from line ten onwards begins with the qualifier
"unless" casting doubt over all that follows. There is no doubt as to the
event, but only its connection to the solitary's mating call. Is this a response?
Does the solitary recognize it as such? If it is a response, then it belongs to
that species of oracular answer in which the supplicant gets what he literally
asks for, as if to teach him the necessary deviousness of erotic fulfillment.

> And nothing ever came of what he cried
> Unless it was the embodiment that crashed
> In the cliff's talus on the other side,
> And then in the far-distant water splashed,
> But after a time allowed for it to swim,
> Instead of proving human when it neared
> And someone else additional to him,
> As a great buck it powerfully appeared,
> Pushing the crumpled water up ahead,
> And landed pouring like a waterfall,
> And stumbled through the rocks with horny tread,
> And forced the underbrush—and that was all.

The Adamic parody is heightened by the way in which the buck's
coming is described. Frost likens it to a heavenly descent, appropriate to a
messenger from the other side: first the creature crashes, then makes its way
from the far-distant shore. And when it finally appears, streaming with
power, its emblematic significance is hard to avoid, though Frost Ameri-
canizes it as a buck, no royal stag, a rough beast standing for nothing other
than its own powerful presence—and that was all. By the end of the poem,
the solitary is measured against Adam, the namer, and Orpheus, the tamer,
of beasts, but neither name nor music issues from his muted lips. Whatever
stature he does achieve comes from this muteness at the close, as he and
the reader stand witness to a rugged appearance of original power.

Whereas the opening line of "The Most of It" records a delusion—
and a weak delusion at that—the beginning of "Never Again Would

Birds' Song Be the Same" presents a central figure (less distinguishable from the poet) capable of recognizing a fable strong and apt enough to inspire belief. Once again, as in "The Most of It," Frost undoes specificity of place; the visionary marker "there," as well as the inclusive "in all the garden round," tells us that we are in the region of no place in particular, the region of Utopia:

> He would declare and could himself believe
> That the birds there in all the garden round
> From having heard the daylong voice of Eve
> Had added to their own an oversound,
> Her tone of meaning but without the words.
> Admittedly an eloquence so soft
> Could only have had an influence on birds
> When call or laughter carried it aloft.
> Be that as may be, she was in their song.
> Moreover her voice upon their voices crossed
> Had now persisted in the woods so long
> That probably it never would be lost.
> Never again would birds' song be the same.
> And to do that to birds was why she came.

Access to Edenic origin in this poem is not hedged about by fear or dread; the spot is not ringed by a *cordon sanitaire*. Access to the spot proceeds through the corridors of belief. The declaring and believing poet gets there on his own, gets there "himself." One reason for this relaxation of the rigors of original pursuit is that the origin, the garden, lies all around us, if we can only hear it in the overtone of the birds, those mocking generations. These are the self-same birds who heard, not the sad voice of Ruth, but the laughing voice of Eve. After all these birds seem to pattern themselves on Eve's daylong voice; they are not nighttime warblers, darkling singers. The "daylong voice of Eve" goes back to the sense of day in "Nothing Gold Can Stay," only here the point is precisely that the golden voice of Eve, voice of the golden age, does indeed stay, or persist, in the birds' song about us. The sense of happy mimicry pervading the poem is picked up in the line "Admittedly an eloquence so soft," where Frost's own lines mimic the soft eloquence of Eve—her tone of meaning, but this time with the words. As we repeat the repeating birds, we experience Eve's influence. Here we approach the idea of an originality available through repetition, repetition seen not as curse but as a form of renewal. In line with this emphasis, Frost has little anxiety about the mixing of human and natural orders, little desire to scrutinize the boundaries of contamination. He merely asserts: "she was in their song." There is no effort to separate realms as in Stevens's "The Idea of Order at Key West." Instead, Frost accepts the crossing of voices: "her voice upon their voices crossed." Suspended in the line's final position, "crossed" raises the specter of conflict, as in a crossing of swords, but Frost raises it only to dispel it. He is interested in a creative crossing, a blending, a warp and woof of voice, creating a seamless verbal tapestry.

The nearly hidden ambiguity of "crossed" gets more openly expressed in the way "Never Again" carries elegiac hints only to undo them. The title (especially its first two words) taken alone, seems to indicate loss; the change it augurs appears to be a change for the worse. But the point of the poem is that what we thought was lost has actually persisted—or "probably" has, to use Frost's own qualifier, if only we know how to read that persistence, how to discover its strands of filiation back to the first story. "Persistence" is a virtue Frost also celebrated at the close of "Sitting by a Bush in Broad Sunlight." One of the subtlest ways Frost finds to undo this elegiac impulse comes again by using enjambment to create an undertone. "Moreover her voice upon their voices crossed / Had now persisted in the woods so long," makes us pause at "so long," only to realize as we read on further that the words mean exactly what they say: the phrase does not mean good-by in this context.

"Never Again" tells us that our route back to the garden runs through Eve, not Adam. We follow her verbal trace. Interestingly, Frost associates Eve not only with song, which would square with the Miltonic account, but also with eloquence, a faculty more often associated with Adam. According to this song, eloquence is song, song eloquence; we are not in the realm of the oven bird, who learns in singing not to sing. If Adam appears at all in this poem, it may be in the guise of the "He" who inaugurates the fable. This would be Frost's true version of the American Adam—not someone who forges his own discourse as if made new, but a singer who is also a listener, a repeater of the sounds of originality.

The poignance of this poem might also have something to do with the fact that it was written soon after Elinor Frost's death. As Frost wrote in a letter: "she has been the unspoken half of everything I ever wrote." This might explain the terms of Eve's influence as described here. So "Never Again Would Birds' Song Be the Same" can also be read as a kind of elegy to Elinor which turns out in the end not to be an elegy at all, because her sound still persists in the sound of the birds: "probably it never would be lost."

IV

From the beginning of "Directive" the movement back toward an earlier time is viewed as a return to simplicity, in the root sense of oneness, that which is not compounded or confused, to draw on the poem's last word. To go back behind—or beyond—confusion is to return to the unity of wholeness. This movement, from the beginning, is seen as a fashioned action—"a time made simple"—and a violent one as well. The simple thing, here at the beginning, is seen not so much as totality, but as a synecdoche, a microcosm. Wholeness is not achieved without the violence of prior fragmentation. And the word "simple" of course carries its negative connotations as well, so that the loss of detail could lead to a damning as well as a saving simplicity, could lead to forgetfulness as much as remembrance. Simplicity here is achieved through the loss of what Frost terms "detail," a word that can be taken in a number of contexts, either as richness or as superfluity. How much of a loss *is* the loss of detail.

And this action of burning, dissolving, breaking off—is it a healing violence, a counter-violence aimed against the wounds of the past? Even before Frost reaches the series of famous paradoxes—"a house that is no more a house..."—the poem is riddled with dark sayings about the nature of this regenerative return to the simple past, filled with the poet's sense of the double nature of what he is doing even as he asserts the triumph of the *simplex*, the single thing that can save us.

Despite its emphasis on wholeness and simplicity, "Directive" also has a kind of division built into it in the form of the split between the narrating guide and his audience. "Let us go then, you and I," goes the poem's implicit beginning; and the poem's action needs an auditor, an interpreter, an other, present at the site, to complete its meaning. One of the poem's many open questions is whether or not narrator and auditor merge at the close in the shared gesture of drinking the waters of the source. The offer is certainly made, but whether or not it is accepted depends upon the reaction of the reader-initiate. Equally unclear is whether the narrator drinks. Is he a guide whose mission is to lead others to a sacred spot he himself is barred from knowing? Or has he already tasted the waters? Poetic tradition certainly offers examples of guides, such as Virgil, or the Ancient Mariner, who can save others but not themselves. One way of saving others is to warn them against the sins of the guide, and in this sense it is worth thinking about the narrator's implication in the scene of ruin he brings us to face. For this site in the woods may also be thought of as a scene of the crime. Indeed, if the allusion to St. Mark's cryptic passage points to the necessity of interpreting parables, then surely one of the poem's prime riddles is what connection can this speaker have to this landscape. To leave the house as merely a generalized example of human decay would seem to solve the riddle too quickly. Why does this speaker take us here? Why is he the only survivor of this house? Where is everyone else? Without joining the biographical debate over Frost's character, I find it perplexing that commentators have not called attention to the ruin of Frost's own "house" in treating the site of "Directive." The grim line "This was no playhouse but a house in earnest" seems to lose all resonance otherwise. Here we have "Home Burial" carried to the extreme: the home, "now slowly closing like a dent in dough," is being buried before our eyes.

Indeed, Frost inscribes himself upon the landscape through a favorite trick: ringing changes on his own name. The spirit of this place is "an enormous Glacier"—"Frost" writ large:

> You must not mind a certain coolness from him
> Still said to haunt this side of Panther Mountain.

As Stevens put it, "Cold is our element," and for Frost there is a kind of mystic attunement, a baptismal bond, between his own name and the waters he calls "Cold as a spring as yet so near its source." To introduce another metaphor, the difficult return to the site resembles the salmon's swim upstream, back to its spawning grounds and its death. Return to the origin can thus itself become the sign of death, death conceived not as alienation but as recognition. Here, the return merges with the great theme of the *nostos*.

As Allen Grossman has pointed out in an essay on Hart Crane and the question of origins, there are two great archetypes of the *nostos* motif:

> One is the return to the remembered place (like Odysseus' return
> to Ithaka); the other is the return to the unremembered place of
> origins (like Socrates' return to the Idea, or Shelley's "Die, / If
> thou woulds't be with that which thou dost seek!"). The return
> to the remembered place through the good use of time leads to
> an enhancement of the mortal self, involving an internalization
> by the voyager of his own past and then its revalidation in the
> external world (recovery of Ithaka and remarriage with Penelope). The return to the unremembered place is by contrast sacrificial, requiring and justifying the destruction of time and the
> self at home in it.

Part of the difficulty posed by "Directive" is the way it seems equally poised between the remembered and the unremembered place. The poem is clearly a journey homeward, but to home as remembered place, or to the home that never was? In this sense the real paradox would run: "There is a house that never was a house." The medicinal or healing drink offered at the end of the poem does not appear to cure the wounds of time within time, for the fragmented debris of the past can never be made whole again. The dishes remain shattered, the grail broken, the house slowly closing. These wounds receive the purgatorial waters of tears, not the purifying waters of the origin: "Weep for what little things could make them glad. / Then for the house that is no more a house." Nor does it appear that a return is possible to the mortal world. It is more a question of returning to the Idea that underlies the temporal house, the idea of the pure stream of the origin, "A brook that was the water of the house." Before one calls this the waters of life, it should be noted that the house fed by this brook is now a ghost house. Indeed, the kind of cold Frost associates with the brook has its correlative in poets such as Stevens and Bishop, where it is a kind of deathly cold, an inhuman cold, a cold inhospitable to human life. There is the cold of "The Snow Man": "One must have a mind of winter . . . And have been cold a long time." And there is the frigid water of Bishop's "At the Fishhouses": "Cold dark deep and absolutely clear, / element bearable to no mortal." For Bishop, one reason the water is "bearable to no mortal" has to do with the fact that it is *absolutely* clear. She means that adverb with dead seriousness. This absoluteness also underscores the danger of the cold in "The Snow Man" and, I would argue, in "Directive" as well, where absolution is achieved only by contact with the absolute, that which Frost describes as "Too lofty and original to rage." But such absolution signifies death as well as life. Within the Christian matrix of paradoxes, we can accept the idea of dying to the world only to live in a transcendent sphere, but does "Directive" sustain such faith? Though the poem is filled with parodic Christian symbolism, best detailed by Marie Borroff, it remains, as Borroff herself writes: "not Christian . . . the revelation the poem brings is moral rather than supernatural." Yet this is a hard morality indeed, hard on others, hard on the self.

The question of the poem's tantalizing allusions to New Testament doctrine culminates, of course, in the reference to the passage in Mark on the role of parable:

> And he said unto them, Unto you it is given to know the mystery of the kingdom of God: but unto them that are without, all these things are done in parables:
> That seeing they may see, and not perceive; and hearing they

may hear, and not understand; lest at any time they should be converted, and their sins should be forgiven them.

Frank Kermode's *The Genesis of Secrecy* takes this passage from Mark as adumbrating the essential condition of interpretive communities:

> In this tradition insiders can hope to achieve correct interpre-
> tation, though their hope may be frequently, perhaps always,
> disappointed; whereas those outside cannot. There is seeing and
> hearing, which are what naive listeners and readers do; and there
> is perceiving and understanding, which are in principle reserved
> to an elect.

It is perhaps this seemingly smug courting of the fit audience, though few, that leads Poirier to complain that the poem's ironies are "consequential" only to those "who have enclosed themselves within the circuit of Frost's own work." There are few other instances of such direct allusion in Frost's poetry, so we have little precedent for how to read such open quotation in his work. "Out, Out—" represents another example and I think interpretation of that poem has suffered for critics taking the allusion with too little sense of its dialectical complexities. The passage from Mark is notoriously "dark" itself and would thus be a strange example to choose in the hope of stabilizing one's meaning. The phrasing of "as Saint Mark says they mustn't," with its prissy tone of smug election, serves to mock rather than enforce any easy distinction between elect and outcast, insider and outsider. And when Frost talks about the "wrong ones," nothing in the poem would lend itself to taking "wrong" as a moral category. After all, the notion of right and wrong is considerably complicated by the fact that the narrator admits to having stolen the goblet.

Poirier asks the crucial question of whether it is *good* to get beyond confusion and surely the answer to this question—if answer is the appropriate response—determines whether one accepts the offered potion. To be "whole" is to return to the unremembered place of origins; it stands in opposition to the remembered place, the slowly closing "hole" of the natural landscape. Such wholeness seems a kind of self-healing, though it cannot reconstitute the ruinous fragments of history or of the self's actions in history. Surveying its own past, the self may stand confused, but this is at least a sign of moral sentience.

The final line of "Directive" will always seem to tear free from context, for what does its action describe if not an escape from the confinement of context and all its confusions? To be untouched by confusion must mean that one is untouched by life and indeed there seems no possibility of return after drinking the potion. Or, if return is possible, it may only be at the cost of becoming confused again. We remain whole only so long as we remain in this spot. Frost brings us to a point where origin and end merge and the story ceases. So does representation: Frost can only call the spring "cold." He has deliberately elided the Keatsian phantasia of the Nightingale Ode, whose magic potion is the wellspring of a gorgeous chain of romance associations, culled from the region of the "warm South," a region not native to Keats and certainly not to Frost. The draught of Keatsian vintage inspires a chain of figurations, whereas Frost's chills language. Keats's flight takes him far away, Frost's to earthward.

For Frost, the enemy of imagination seems to be "confusion," the loss of self in a proliferation of motives, deeds, and events that carry one far from both the remembered place (the home) and the unremembered place of origin. But return to that place of fabricated wholeness can also destroy the imagination. Confronted with the evidence of his actions, the ruins of his historical house, the poet might indeed have given himself up to that "rage" (etymologically, "madness") which it is the presumed power of the spring to cure. As it is, the poem shows us Frost succumbing neither to madness nor to radical cure: the cup is suspended, the spring as yet but "so near" its source. This saving distance from the source is also a form of salvation: the necessary scepticism that keeps one from drowning in one's own fiction.

Chronology

<table>
<tr><td>1874</td><td>Robert Frost is born on March 26 in San Francisco, California to William Prescott Frost, Jr., and Isabelle Moodie Frost.</td></tr>
<tr><td>1874–84</td><td>Frost spends his childhood in San Francisco.</td></tr>
<tr><td>1885</td><td>After the death of his father, Frost moves to Lawrence, Massachusetts, with his mother and sister.</td></tr>
<tr><td>1892</td><td>Graduates from Lawrence High School with his co-valedictorian and future wife, Elinor White. He attends Dartmouth College for a few months.</td></tr>
<tr><td>1893</td><td>Frost takes his first teaching job (8th grade) in Methuen, Massachusetts. He works in the Arlington Mill in Lawrence.</td></tr>
<tr><td>1894</td><td>"My Butterfly," Frost's first published poem, appears in The Independent.</td></tr>
<tr><td>1895</td><td>Frost marries Elinor Miriam White.</td></tr>
<tr><td>1896</td><td>Their first son, Eliot, is born.</td></tr>
<tr><td>1897–99</td><td>Frost attends Harvard as an undergraduate.</td></tr>
<tr><td>1899</td><td>Frost's daughter Lesley is born.</td></tr>
<tr><td>1900</td><td>Eliot Frost dies. Another son, Carol, is born. The family moves to a farm in Derry, New Hampshire.</td></tr>
<tr><td>1900–10</td><td>Years of farming and teaching at the Pinkerton Academy in Derry.</td></tr>
<tr><td>1903</td><td>Daughter Irma is born.</td></tr>
<tr><td>1905</td><td>Daughter Marjorie is born.</td></tr>
</table>

1907	Daughter Elinor Bettina is born; dies in infancy.
1911–12	Frost teaches psychology at New Hampshire State Normal School in Plymouth.
1912–15	Residence in England with Elinor and their four children. Frost writes and farms in Buckinghamshire and Herefordshire. Meets Ezra Pound.
1913	*A Boy's Will* is published in London. Frost meets Edward Thomas.
1914	*North of Boston* is published in London.
1915	The Frosts return from England and move to a farm in Franconia, New Hampshire. Frost's two books are published in the U.S.
1916	*Mountain Interval* is published. Frost reads as Phi Beta Kappa Poet at Harvard and is elected to the National Institute of Arts and Letters.
1917	Frost begins teaching English at Amherst College.
1919	Moves to new farm near South Shaftsbury, Vermont.
1920	Co-founds the Breadloaf School of English at Middlebury College.
1921–23	Frost is Poet in Residence at the University of Michigan.
1923	*Selected Poems* and *New Hampshire* are published.
1923–25	Serves as Professor of English at Amherst College.
1924	Receives the Pulitzer Prize for *New Hampshire*.
1925–26	Frost is Fellow in Letters at the University of Michigan.
1926	Resumes teaching at Amherst College.
1928	*West-Running Brook* is published.
1929	*A Way Out* is published. Robert and Elinor move to Gully Farm in Bennington, Vermont.
1930	*Collected Poems* is published.
1934	Frost's daughter, Marjorie Frost Fraser, dies.

1936   *A Further Range* is published. Frost serves as Charles Eliot Norton Professor of Poetry at Harvard University.

1937   Receives his second Pulitzer Prize for *A Further Range.*

1938   Elinor White Frost dies. Frost resigns from Amherst College.

1939   The enlarged *Collected Poems* is published. Frost is awarded the National Institute of Arts and Letters Gold Medal for Poetry. Buys a farm in Ripton, Vermont, for a summer home.

1939–42 Serves as Ralph Waldo Emerson Fellow in Poetry at Harvard.

1940   Frost's son Carol commits suicide.

1942   *A Witness Tree* is published.

1943   Frost receives his third Pulitzer Prize for *A Witness Tree.* Becomes Ticknor Fellow in the Humanities at Dartmouth College.

1945   *A Masque of Reason* is published.

1947   *Steeple Bush* and *A Masque of Mercy* are published.

1949   *Complete Poems* is published.

1950   The U.S. Senate passes a resolution commending Frost on the event of his seventy-fifth birthday.

1954   Frost celebrates his eightieth birthday with a reception at the White House. He represents the U.S. at the World Congress of Writers in Sao Paulo, Brazil.

1957   Frost travels to England, where he is honored at Oxford and Cambridge Universities and the National University of Ireland. Dines with President Eisenhower at the White House.

1958   Appointed Consultant in Poetry to the Library of Congress.

1959 Frost's eighty-fifth birthday is marked by another U.S. Senate commendation and Lionel Trilling's speech "A Cultural Episode."

1961 Frost reads "The Gift Outright" at the Inauguration of President John F. Kennedy. Lectures in Athens and Jerusalem.

1962 Frost visits Moscow as a guest of the Soviet Government. He meets privately with Premier Khrushchev; reads "Mending Wall." *In the Clearing* is published.

1963 Frost is awarded the Bollingen Prize for Poetry. He dies on January 29 in Boston.

Contributors

HAROLD BLOOM, Sterling Professor of the Humanities at Yale University, is the author of *The Anxiety of Influence, Poetry and Repression*, and many other volumes of literary criticism. His forthcoming study, *Freud: Transference and Authority*, attempts a full-scale reading of all of Freud's major writings. A MacArthur Prize Fellow, he is general editor of five series of literary criticism published by Chelsea House.

ROBERT PACK, Abernathy Professor of Literature at Middlebury College, is a poet and the director of the Breadloaf Writers' Conference. His books of poetry include *Waking to My Name* and *Faces in a Single Tree*, and he is the author of *Affirming Limits: Essays on Mortality, Choice, and Poetic Form*.

FRANK LENTRICCHIA is Autrey Professor of Humanities at Rice University. He is the author of *Robert Frost: Modern Poetics and the Landscapes of Self*, *After the New Criticism*, and *Criticism and Social Change*.

RICHARD POIRIER is Distinguished Professor of English at Rutgers University and editor of *Raritan*. His books of criticism include *The Performing Self* and *Robert Frost: The Work of Knowing*.

MARIE BORROFF is William Lampson Professor of English at Yale University. She is the author of *Language and the Poet: Verbal Artistry in Frost, Stevens, and Moore* and *Sir Gawain and the Green Knight: A Stylistic and Metrical Study*.

SYDNEY LEA is Professor of English at the University of Massachusetts and the editor of *The New England Review and Breadloaf Quarterly*.

171

DAVID BROMWICH is Professor of English at Princeton University. He is the author of *Hazlitt: The Mind of a Critic.*

HERBERT MARKS is Assistant Professor of Comparative Literature at the University of Indiana and the author of a number of essays on the Bible and modern poetry.

CHARLES BERGER is Associate Professor of English at Yale University. He is the author of *Forms of Farewell: The Late Poetry of Wallace Stevens.*

Bibliography

Abel, Darrel. "Robert Frost's 'True Make-Believe.' " *Texas Studies in Literature and Language* 20, no. 4 (1978): 552–78.

Auden, W. H. "Robert Frost." In *The Dyer's Hand and Other Essays*, 337–53. New York: Random House, 1962.

Bacon, Helen. "In- and Outdoor Schooling." In *Robert Frost: Lectures on the Centennial of His Birth*. Washington, D.C.: Library of Congress, 1975.

Baker, Carlos. "Frost on the Pumpkin." In *The Echoing Green*, 186–212. Princeton: Princeton University Press, 1984.

Barry, Elaine. *Robert Frost*. New York: Frederick Ungar, 1973.

Berger, Harry, Jr. "Poetry as Revision: Interpreting Robert Frost." *Criticism* 10 (1968): 1–22.

Bogan, Louise. "Robert Frost." In *A Poet's Alphabet*, 160–63. New York: McGraw-Hill, 1970.

Brower, Reuben A. *The Poetry of Robert Frost: Constellations of Intention*. New York: Oxford University Press, 1963.

Carruth, Hayden. "The New-England Tradition." In *Regional Perspectives: An Examination of America's Literary Heritage*, edited by John G. Burke, 1–48. Chicago: American Library Association, 1973.

Cook, Reginald L. *The Dimensions of Robert Frost*. New York: Rinehart, 1958.

———. *Robert Frost: A Living Voice*. Amherst: University of Massachusetts Press, 1974.

Cowley, Malcolm. "Robert Frost: A Dissenting Opinion." In *A Many-Windowed House*, 201–12. Carbondale: Southern Illinois University Press, 1970.

Cox, James M., ed. *Robert Frost: A Collection of Critical Essays*. Englewood Cliffs, N.J.: Prentice-Hall, 1962.

Cox, Sidney. *A Swinger of Birches*. New York: New York University Press, 1960.

Dendinger, Lloyd N. "The Ghost-Haunted Woodland of Robert Frost." *South Atlantic Bulletin* 38 (1973): 87–94.

Dickey, James. "Robert Frost." In *Babel to Byzantium: Poets and Poetry Now*, 200–9. New York: Farrar, Straus and Giroux, 1968.

Donoghue, Denis. "Robert Frost." In *Connoisseurs of Chaos: Ideas of Order in Modern American Poetry*. New York: Macmillan, 1965.

Dowell, Peter W. "Counter-Images and Their Function in the Poetry of Robert Frost." *Tennessee Studies in Literature* 14 (1969): 15–30.

Doyle, John Robert, Jr. *The Poetry of Robert Frost.* Johannesburg: Witwatersrand University Press, 1962.

Eberhart, Richard. "Robert Frost in the Clearing." *Southern Review* 11 (Spring 1975): 260–68.

Gerber, Philip C. *Robert Frost.* New York: Twayne Publishers, 1966.

Gould, Jean. *Robert Frost: The Aim Was Song.* New York: Dodd, Mead, and Co., 1964.

Greenberg, Robert A., and James G. Hepburn, eds. *Robert Frost: An Introduction.* New York: Holt, Rinehart, and Winston, 1961.

Harris, Kathryn Gibbs, ed. *Robert Frost: Studies of the Poetry.* Boston: G. K. Hall and Co., 1979.

Haynes, Donald T. "The Narrative Unity of *A Boy's Will.*" *PMLA* 137 (1972): 452–64.

Howe, Irving. "Robert Frost: A Momentary Stay." In *A World More Attractive,* 144–57. New York: Horizon Press, 1963.

Irwin, W. R. "The Unity of Frost's Masques." *American Literature* 32 (1960): 302–12.

Isaacs, Elizabeth. *An Introduction to Robert Frost.* Denver: Alan Swallow, 1962.

Jarrell, Randall. "The Other Frost" and "To the Laodiceans." In *Poetry and the Age,* 28–36, 37–69. New York: Alfred A. Knopf, 1953.

Jennings, Elizabeth. *Frost.* New York: Barnes and Noble, 1966.

Kemp, John C. *Robert Frost and New England: The Poet as Regionalist.* Princeton: Princeton University Press, 1979.

Kennedy, John F. "Poetry and Power." *Atlantic Monthly* 213 (February 1964): 53–54.

Lathem, Edward Connery, ed. *A Concordance to the Poetry of Robert Frost.* New York: Holt Information Systems, 1971.

Lentricchia, Frank. *Robert Frost: Modern Poetics and the Landscapes of Self.* Durham, N.C.: Duke University Press, 1975.

———. "Robert Frost: The Aesthetics of Voice and the Theory of Poetry." *Criticism* 15 (Winter 1973): 28–42.

Lynen, John F. *The Pastoral Art of Robert Frost.* New Haven: Yale University Press, 1960.

———. "The Poet's Meaning and the Poem's World." In *Modern Poetry,* edited by John Hollander, 485–500. New York: Oxford University Press, 1968.

Michaels, Walter Benn. "Getting Physical." *Raritan* 2, no. 2 (Fall 1982): 103–13.

Morrison, Theodore. "Frost: Country Poet and Cosmopolitan Poet." *Yale Review* 59 (1970): 179–96.

Nagel, James, and Richard Astro, eds. *American Literature: The New England Heritage.* New York: Garland Publishing, 1981.

Nitchie, George W. *Human Values in the Poetry of Robert Frost.* Durham, N.C.: Duke University Press, 1960.

Pearce, Roy Harvey. *The Continuity of American Poetry.* Princeton: Princeton University Press, 1961.

———. "Frost's Momentary Stay." *Kenyon Review* 23 (Spring 1961): 258–73.

Poirier, Richard. "Frost, Winnicott, Burke." *Raritan* 2, no. 2 (Fall 1982): 114–27.

———. *Robert Frost: The Work of Knowing.* New York: Oxford University Press, 1977.

Potter, James L. *Robert Frost Handbook*. University Park: The Pennsylvania State University Press, 1980.

Pritchard, William. *Frost: A Literary Life Reconsidered*. New York: Oxford University Press, 1984.

———. "Wildness of Logic in Modern Lyric," In *Forms of Lyric: Selected Papers from the English Institute*, edited by Reuben A. Brower. New York: Columbia University Press, 1970.

———. "The Grip of Frost." *Hudson Review* 29, no. 2 (Summer 1976): 185–204.

Ryan, Alvan S. "Frost and Emerson: Voice and Vision." *Massachusetts Review* 1 (1959): 5–23.

Sabin, Margery. "The Fate of the Frost Speaker." *Raritan* 2, no. 2 (Fall 1982): 128–39.

Seargeant, Elizabeth Shepley. *Robert Frost: The Trial by Existence*. New York: Holt, Rinehart, and Winston, 1960.

Sears, John F. "The Subversive Performer in Frost's 'Snow' and 'Out, Out—.'" In *The Motive for Metaphor*, edited by Francis Blessington. Boston: Northeastern University Press, 1983.

———. "William James, Henri Bergson, and the Poetics of Robert Frost." *New England Quarterly* 48 (1975): 341–61.

Simpson, Lewis P., ed. *Profile of Robert Frost*. Columbus, Ohio: Charles E. Merrill, 1971.

Smythe, Daniel. *Robert Frost Speaks*. New York: Twayne Publishers, 1964.

Sohn, David A. and Richard Tyre. *Frost: The Poet and His Poetry*. New York: Holt, Rinehart, and Winston, 1967.

Squires, Radcliffe. *The Major Themes of Robert Frost*. Ann Arbor: University of Michigan Press, 1963.

Sutton, William A., ed. *Newdick's Season of Frost*. Albany: State University of New York Press, 1976.

Tharpe, Jac L., ed. *Frost: Centennial Essays*. Jackson: University Press of Mississippi, 1974.

———. *Frost: Centennial Essays II*. Jackson: University Press of Mississippi, 1976.

———. *Frost: Centennial Essays III*. Jackson: University Press of Mississippi, 1978.

Thompson, Lawrance. *Fire and Ice: The Art and Thought of Robert Frost*. New York: Holt, Rinehart, and Winston, 1942.

———. *Robert Frost: The Early Years, 1874–1915*. New York: Holt, Rinehart, and Winston, 1966.

———. *Robert Frost: The Years of Triumph, 1915–1938*. New York: Holt, Rinehart, and Winston, 1970.

Traschen, Isadore. "Robert Frost: Some Divisions in a Whole Man." *Yale Review* 55 (Autumn 1965): 57–70.

Trilling, Lionel. "A Speech on Robert Frost: A Cultural Episode." *Partisan Review* 26 (Summer 1959): 445–52.

Untermeyer, Louis. *Robert Frost: A Backward Look* (lecture). Washington, D.C.: Library of Congress, 1964.

Vander Ven, Tom. "Robert Frost's Dramatic Principle of 'Oversound.'" *American Literature* 45 (1973): 238–51.

Vitelli, James R. "Robert Frost: The Contrarieties of Talent and Tradition." *New England Quarterly* 47 (1974): 351–67.

Waggoner, Hyatt H. "The Strategic Retreat." In *American Poets: From the Puritans to the Present*. Boston: Houghton Mifflin, 1968.

Warren, Robert Penn. "The Themes of Robert Frost." In *Selected Essays*, 118–36. New York: Random House, 1958.

Watts, Harold H. "Robert Frost and the Interrupted Dialogue." *American Literature* 27 (March 1955): 69–87.

Winters, Yvor. "Robert Frost: Or, The Spiritual Drifter as Poet." In *The Function of Criticism*, 157–88. Denver: Alan Swallow, 1957.

Acknowledgments

Poetry appearing throughout the volume by Robert Frost from *The Poetry of Robert Frost* edited by Edward Connery Lathem © 1916, 1923, 1928, 1934, 1947, 1949, 1969 by Holt, Rinehart and Winston. © 1942, 1944, 1948, 1951, 1956, 1962 by Robert Frost. © 1970, 1975, 1976 by Lesley Frost Ballantine. Reprinted by permission of Henry Holt and Company.

"Frost's Enigmatical Reserve: The Poet as Teacher and Preacher" by Robert Pack from *Affirming Limits: Essays on Mortality, Choice, and Poetic Form* by Robert Pack, ©1985 by The University of Massachusetts Press. (Originally delivered in 1974 and published in *Robert Frost: Lectures on the Centennial of His Birth* [Washington, D.C.: Library of Congress, 1975].) Reprinted by permission.

"The Redemptive Imagination" by Frank Lentricchia from *Robert Frost: Modern Poetics and the Landscapes of Self* by Frank Lentricchia, ©1975 by Duke University Press. Reprinted by permission.

"Choices" by Richard Poirier from *Robert Frost: The Work of Knowing* by Richard Poirier, ©1977 by Oxford University Press, Inc. Reprinted by permission.

"Robert Frost's New Testament: The Uses of Simplicity" by Marie Borroff from *Language and the Poet: Verbal Artistry in Frost, Stevens, and Moore* by Marie Borroff, ©1979 by The University of Chicago. Reprinted by permission of The University of Chicago Press.

"From Sublime to Rigamarole: Relations of Frost to Wordsworth" by Sydney Lea from *Studies in Romanticism* 19, no.1 (Spring 1980), ©1980 by the Trustees of Boston University. Reprinted by permission.

"Wordsworth, Frost, Stevens and the Poetic Vocation" by David Bromwich from *Studies in Romanticism* 21, no.1 (Spring 1982), ©1982 by the Trustees of Boston University. Reprinted by permission.

"The Counter-Intelligence of Robert Frost" by Herbert Marks from *The Yale Review* 71, no.4 (Summer 1982), ©1982 by Yale University. Reprinted by permission of the author and *The Yale Review*.

"Echoing Eden: Frost and Origins" by Charles Berger, ©1986 by Charles Berger. Published for the first time in this volume. Printed by permission.

Index